D1452536

THE POSSIBILITY OF AN ALL-KNOWING GOD

The Possibility of an All-Knowing God

Jonathan L. Kvanvig

Assistant Professor of Philosophy
Texas A & M University

St. Martin's Press   New York

First published in the United States of America in 1986

Printed in Hong Kong

ISBN 0–312–63195–2

Library of Congress Cataloging-in-Publication Data
Kvanvig, Jonathan L.
The possibility of an all-knowing God.
Bibliography: p.
Includes index.
1. God—Omniscience.   I. Title.
BT131.K86   1986   231′.4   86–6465
ISBN 0–312–63195–2

To Carol June, whose commitment, support and comfort
makes possible that which was not

Contents

vii

Introduction

Christians and other theists have long held that God is omniscient. Perhaps nowhere is the claim that God's knowledge is incomparable more eloquently stated than in Psalm 139, from which the following is taken (New International Version):

> O Lord, you have searched me
> and you know me.
> You know when I sit and when I rise;
> you perceive my thoughts from afar.
> You discern my going out and my lying down;
> you are familiar with all my ways.
> Before a word is on my tongue
> you know it completely, O Lord.
>
> You hem me in, behind and before;
> you have laid your hand upon me.
> Such knowledge is too wonderful for me,
> too lofty for me to attain.
>
> If I say, 'Surely the darkness will hide me
> and the light become night around me,'
> even the darkness will not be dark to you;
> the night will shine like the day,
> for darkness is as light to you.

Though we should show care in imputing theological formulae to Biblical writers, it is difficult to avoid seeing a clear statement here that God knows all there is to know, for there is nothing which is hid from Him.

Not only are such thoughts fitting of the majesty of God, there are many other characteristics of God which seem to require something at least very close to omniscience. Christians take God to be actively involved in forming a certain sort of character in them, yet in order to avoid error in so forming our characters, God must know both what we are like to start with and what effect certain events will have on our character. Further, if God is to be perfectly just, He must fail to lack any knowledge relevant to the judgements which He gives. Perhaps a somewhat ignorant judge could avoid being blameworthy for any of his decisions based on ignorance; however, perfect justice requires a more perfect knowledge.

There are religious and psychological motivations for the doctrine of omniscience as well. Theists not only ask for Divine intervention in the course of human affairs, they also seek Divine guidance in conducting their affairs. Further, in asking for such guidance, the proper attitude towards God is one of complete trust and confidence in the truth of what He communicates. Such an attitude would be misplaced were it to turn out that sometimes what God claims is not true (though, of course, this is not to deny that humans can mistakenly take God to have claimed something which He has not in fact claimed).

The doctrine of omniscience is also of psychological significance. Humans have a deep need to be unconditionally loved, to be loved in spite of lack of achievement, moral failure, and various sorts of other inadequacies. To find such unconditional love in one's relationship with one's Creator depends at least on an inability to hide from Him what we tend to hide from each other. For God to love us absolutely and unconditionally in the way He claims to requires that nothing within our make-up be hid from His awareness.

There are also more philosophical motivations for a theist to hold that God is omniscient. The Anselmian conception of God, that He is that than which a greater cannot be conceived, generates an easy proof that if God exists He must be omniscient. For if there were a being taken to be God, but was less than omniscient, that being would be undeserving of the title 'God', for being omniscient is a great-making property and is thus a property which God must have. Any being lacking that property might have many impressive qualities, but his being such that it is possible for some other being to be greater than he entails that his greatness is not sufficient to allow him access to the Divine Office. One deserves to occupy the Divine Office, one deserves the title 'God', only if (and if) one is a being of whom a greater is not possible.

These motivations lead straightforwardly to an affirmation of the doctrine of omniscience, and they also lead to a natural construal of that doctrine. Intuitively, we might say that the claim that God is omniscient is the claim that God knows everything. And what are the things which are known? A common answer, though not the only one, is that God knows everything that is true. There is nothing true that He is unaware of, and He does not make any mistakes about what is true or not.

Such considerations, then, prompt both an affirmation of the doctrine and a certain construal of the doctrine; and, to this point, there does not seem to be much of philosophical significance about which to be concerned. Yet, complexities quickly arise. First, Anselmian motivations that prompt affirmation of the claim that God is omniscient also prompt affirmation of the claim that no matter how things were to turn out, God would still be omniscient. It is also no mere coincidence that God is omniscient; His majesty and excellence are so great that He simply could not fail to be omniscient.

Yet, if God is essentially omniscient, it follows that He simply could not be mistaken about anything, i.e. He has infallible knowledge. This implication raises problems concerning knowledge of the future. Since we know the future, if we know it at all, on inductive evidence, God's knowledge of the future would have to be quite different in order to be infallible, for inductive grounds never provide for such certainty.

Perhaps it might be suggested that God "sees" the future just as He sees the past and present. Such a response raises considerable ontological worries, for it would seem that the future does not exist to be seen (if it exists at all) – it can perhaps be predicted, but not perceived (until it becomes present).

So one pressing issue that arises is how God can infallibly know the future. A solution could be found if the future were determined by the present, yet this response raises other sorts of difficulties given other views which many Christians accept. For it has seemed to many Christians that an adequate response to the problem of evil must include the free will response: it was better for God to create creatures that are free and sin than to create robot-like creatures lacking freedom who never sin. But if humans are free in an anti-deterministic sense, then at least some of the future is not determined by the present. Hence, the problem of how God infallibly knows the future, especially the free actions of persons, remains.

These motivations for investigating the doctrine of omniscience are of a fairly traditional variety. Recently, though, other motivations have arisen for thinking about the doctrine. First, there has been an increasing tendency to think that the doctrine of omniscience is incompatible with certain other classical doctrines, such as the timelessness and immutability doctrines. As important as these issues concerning the relation between the doctrine of omniscience and other doctrines are, they are of secondary importance to more recent, internal challenges to the traditional doctrine of omniscience described above. These serious internal challenges have arisen from recent investigation of the nature of our awareness of objects around us and awareness of ourselves. These challenges cast doubt, not on the co-tenability of the doctrine of omniscience with other classical doctrines, but rather on the formulation of the doctrine and its very coherence.

These latter worries seem at times to involve only a denial of reductionism concerning the objects of knowledge. On the traditional version of the doctrine above, the object of knowledge is always a proposition. The worries referred to above often seem to call only for an abandoning of reductionism. In other words, the claim often seems to be only that there are types of awareness which are not directed at true claims about the world; rather, some awarenesses are awarenesses of objects, other awarenesses are awarenesses of oneself. Moreover, these latter sorts of awarenesses are not reducible to awareness that a certain claim is true.

As work has progressed on the nature of other- and self-awareness, the challenges that have arisen are more serious than it at first seemed. To some, it has seemed that the proper solution is to hold that there are some things about oneself of which only oneself can be aware. Such conclusions pose problems much more serious than those calling for only minor revisions of the statement of the doctrine, for if it is true that there are things about myself that only I can know or be aware of then there is a clear sense in which I know myself better than God does or can. If this problem is only a minor one, it cannot initially be taken as such.

In spite of the various problems with the traditional construal of omniscience given earlier (that construal which roughly claims that a being is omniscient just in case that being knows everything that is true), I am convinced that this construal remains the proper construal of the doctrine. Yet, the conglomeration of problems which surrounds the traditional construal calls for, I suggest, an extended investigation of the nature of the doctrine of omniscience as well as for a defence of the doctrine. The issues presented raise difficult questions concerning, first, the adequacy of the traditional construal, but also concerning the possibility of any adequate construal of the doctrine. Some of these problems are compatibility problems: for example, there is, of course, a vast amount of literature on the compatibility between divine fore-knowledge and human freedom; and recent literature has included discussions of the relations between omniscience and such other classical attributes as immutability and timelessness. We shall have a chance to look at these issues here as well; but in the face of the multitude of issues which the problems of the doctrine have raised, it is advisable to begin with the doctrine itself. Before determining if omniscience is compatible with other doctrines or well-established beliefs, we should begin by investigating the nature of omniscience itself.

The nature of omniscience is intimately connected with the nature of knowledge, for an omniscient being is just a being with a particular collection of instances of knowledge. So, in order to be clear about omniscience, we must do some investigation into the nature of knowledge. The topics I shall discuss shall be carefully circumscribed, for my intent is not to present a work on epistemology. In particular, I shall not discuss issues in basic epistemology which have only minor impact on the doctrine of omniscience. For example, there are alternative reductive accounts regarding the objects of knowledge to the propositional account, but should such accounts be preferable to the propositional account, the alterations called for in the doctrine of omniscience are obvious and minimal. To be omniscient would still be to know everything; it is just that a different construal of what 'everything' refers to that would have to be accepted. However, when reductionism is challenged (as it has been in recent years), it becomes an interesting question how the doctrine of omniscience must be altered if the challenges succeed; and, if the challenges fail, that too is a topic bearing centrally on the doctrine of omniscience and hence needs to be discussed here. My point is cautionary: my intent is not to provide a complete epistemology to underpin the construal of omniscience I have called the traditional doctrine, but rather to take up those issues in basic epistemology which call for more than trivial changes in the doctrine I intend to defend.

Since the challenges to the doctrine of omniscience arise out of worries concerning God's knowledge of (parts of) the future, a good place to begin is with an investigation of that sort of knowledge, to show that there is a future to be known and that any omniscient being must know all the future.

In addition, we must consider what it is that is known when something is known. The assumption throughout most of the history of philosophy is that some sort of reductive account is to be preferred, and the course of that history has led in an arguably justified way to the view that what we know are propositions or statements which are defined as the sorts of things that are true or false. If this view is false, then of course the doctrine must be altered. However, if some other reductive view takes the place of the propositional view, the alterations are minimal; hence, given the scope of this work, I do not intend to discuss alternative reductive accounts to the propositional one. Recently, though, a considerable literature has arisen claiming that a propositional view of knowledge (or belief) is inadequate precisely because that view is a reductive one. The claim is made that in addition to propositional, or *de dicto*, belief, there is also *de re* and *de se* belief. *De re* belief is belief with a thing as the object of belief. So, for example, it is one thing to believe that the proposition *the tallest spy is a spy* is true; and quite another thing to believe of the tallest spy himself that he is a spy. Finally, it is perhaps one thing to believe of a person in the mirror that his pants are on fire; and quite another to be aware that that person is oneself and to believe of oneself (*de se*) that one's own pants are on fire. There is at least the suggestion of plausibility here that one cannot know everything there is to know if one is limited to propositions as the objects of one's awareness. So in Chapter 2 I shall discuss the issue concerning what it is that is known.

Once we understand knowledge properly, we can turn to God's knowledge. First, I shall discuss the objection to the doctrine of omniscience that arises from God's foreknowledge. I shall defend in Chapter 1 that the future can be known, and that any omniscient being must know the future. Thus, I must face the long-standing objection that if God knows what creatures will do, they cannot be free; and if creatures are free, then God cannot know what they will do. Chapter 3 will be a discussion of these issues.

Even granting that we can extricate ourselves from the logical incompatibility between foreknowledge and freedom, there still remains the question concerning how God does in fact know the future, in particular the future actions of free individuals. For, even if we can show that knowing the future does not imply that no human is free, that provides no explanation of how God can know what a free individual will do. As outlined above, a prime motivator in philosophical concern over the doctrine of omniscience is the issue concerning how God can know future free actions. Now, one way to express this worry is to offer incompatibility arguments: arguments which are intended to prove that if God knows what a person will do, then that person cannot act freely. Yet, the fundamental worry is not necessarily an incompatibility worry. Rather, as I see it, the basic issue is an inability to understand how God could know future free actions, and merely refuting incompatibility arguments does nothing to alleviate this concern. What is needed in addition is a positive account of how God could know what free creatures will do; hence, Chapter 4 will be devoted to providing such a positive account.

Finally, Chapter 5 will be devoted to an investigation of the relationships between omniscience, timelessness, immutability and omnipresence. Critics have recently charged that not all these doctrines are consistent and hence that at least one, perhaps more, must be given up. An investigation of these issues will close our examination of the doctrine of omniscience.

I owe a great deal to others for their help, through discussion or through comments on earlier versions of this manuscript. First, the philosophy departments at the University of Notre Dame, where I first began to think about these issues, and Texas A & M University, where I completed the task, deserve special thanks for the multitude of ways in which they have contributed to this work. In addition, there are some individuals that deserve special mention. In particular, I wish to express my thanks to Robert Burch, Richard Foley, Peter Markie, Hugh McCann, Thomas Morris, Scott Sturgeon, Edward Weirenga, and Linda Zagzebski.

JONATHAN L. KVANVIG

1 The Range of Knowledge

INTRODUCTION

Each of us exists in a particular region of space and time, with every other region of space and time being more or less distant from our own. In addition, our knowledge of the world is pretty much as localised in space and time as is our existence: we know most about the here and now, and much less about the there and then. In order for us to be omniscient, we would have to know not only about our own particular region, but about every other region as well, that is, in order to be omnisicient, a being must have maximal knowledge. The issue of the range of knowledge is what regions, other than the here and now, exist to be known. The spacial issue is not pressing; there are many other places than where I am, and in order to be omniscient, a being must know about all (and all about) those places. The temporal issues are a bit more complex. In addition to the present, there is at least the past, and any omniscient being must know the past; but many have balked at allowing that the future has the same status. Worries over knowledge of the future can be either metaphysical or epistemological. One might think that there is literally nothing 'there' that can be an object of knowledge, or alternatively one might think that though there is a future which we can hope for, hold beliefs about, and ponder over, we can never achieve knowledge regarding it. In either case, the view being defended is that the future is of a different status than the past or present: whereas we can know the past and present, we cannot know the future. This chapter will be an investigation of the epistemological and metaphysical reasons for claiming that the future cannot be known.

It is important to note that there is a strong presumption against the view that severs the ties between omniscience and knowledge of the future. This assumption is important because, in cases where there is such a presumption, showing that there is no good argument against that for which there is such a presumption is sufficient for showing that the claim in question is justified. Thus, if we can show that there is no good argument for severing the tie between omniscience and know-

1

ledge of the future, then we will have given sufficient reason for thinking that omnisicence requires knowledge of the future.

The presumption referred to above arises from the fact that there are strong intuitions on behalf of the view that the future can be the object of knowledge and other intentional attitudes and that it must be known in order for a being to be omniscient. For example, God is clearly portrayed in Scripture as knowing the future. First, He communicates what will occur at various times to his prophets. Further, these predictions are not always dependent on His will; He does not say that they will occur because He has ordained that they occur. In fact, many of the predictions in the Old Testament are clearly of the sort that God wishes would not occur. For instance, the predictions of the unfaithfulness of the Israelites are clearly of this sort. Thus, there seems to be some precedent for holding that God does know the future, and must in order to be omniscient.

Further, human beings surely seem to have the future as the object of their intentional attitudes. We worry over it, hope for it, ponder it, and plan for it. We also seem to know quite a bit about it. To take an example, I surely seem to know that I will go home today at three o'clock, just as I seem to know that I went home yesterday at three o'clock. Of course, the way in which I know the former is different from the way in which I know the latter, but that is not to the point here. The point is that the reality of the future seems to be implied by the fact that we know about it, worry about it, wonder what it will bring, etc.; that we worry over it and take other attitudes towards it seems to indicate that it is "there" in some sense.

In spite of these forceful intuitions, many have remained unconvinced of the possibility of knowledge of the future and have offered arguments against the claims that the future is real and can be known. Before investigating these arguments there are two preliminary topics, a discussion of which will aid us in understanding the issue before us.

PRELIMINARY REMARKS

The first issue has to do with the ontological commitment that a view that the future is real carries. Some claim that the future cannot be real because if it were it would be the present, not the future. Against some views about the ontology of the future, this argument may be a good one. For example, some think that the history of the world is composed of events, some receding into the past, others present, and still others moving towards us from the future. It is not wholly implausible to think that such a view is subject to the above criticism, especially since there are problems allowing that there are such things as non-occurrent events. If all events are occurrent and if the future consists of events moving towards us, those events must also be occurrent, i.e. present events.

I do not wish to describe the future as a set of events moving towards us in time. I propose that we understand talk about the future solely in propositional terms. Grammatically, when we take some attitude (believing, hoping, wishing, etc.) towards the future, the object of the attitude is a that-clause: we believe *that* tomorrow will be a brighter day. What are expressed by such that-clauses are propositions. Thus, talk about the future should not be conceived as requiring the existence of such strange entities as non-occurrent events; it is rather talk about propositions and their truth values. (Of course, if the proposition is true, then there *will be* an event in virtue of which the proposition is true; but this claim does not commit one to the existence of a non-occurrence event – in fact it does not commit one to the (present) existence of any event at all.)

To such a view of the future the above objection is clearly unfounded; there is nothing about this description of the ontology of the future that would require it to be present if real. In fact, it is distinctive of this view of the future that it expressly denies that there are any such things as future events (though there will be events in the future) or future individuals (though, again, there will be individuals in the future). The propositions in question, if true, are true *now*, but the content of the proposition is about what will happen, not what is happening.

The second point of note about the issue of the reality of the future is that it needs to be kept distinct from the issue about whether the future is determined or not. Perhaps some or even most of the future is determined in that there are, in the present, causally sufficient conditions for what will occur. Yet, even for those parts of the future that are so determined, one need not be a realist. One can hold that the future is both not real and yet determined.

Further, one can also believe that some parts of the future are real and yet indeterminate. This claim partially presupposes some later discussion, for there are many philosophers who have argued that some sort of determinism follows from allowing that the future is real. Even so, at least this much is true: the claim that the future is real is not the same claim as that the future is determined; hence, it must be shown that there is an entailment relation between the two, if one thinks there is. When examining the issue of the reality of the future, then, one cannot simply assume that an anti-realist position about the future follows from the fact that the future, or at least some parts of it, are undetermined. We ought to resist identifying the reality of the future with its indeterminacy.

Some may think that this restriction makes the topic of this chapter somewhat less important than it would be if it discussed the connections between indeterminacy and anti-realist views. Perhaps that is so, and perhaps the issue of the reality of the future will only be settled once we examine fully such connections in a later chapter. For those who think the most pressing arguments for being an anti-realist come from indeterminacy considerations, I merely ask that I be allowed to investigate other sorts of reasons for anti-realism in this chapter and to conclude provisionally that anti-realism is unfounded if there are no such arguments. Of course, if the connections some have claimed between indeterminacy and anti-realism cannot be undermined later, this provisional conclusion will have to be abandoned; all I ask is that the reader wait until that discussion has been concluded to judge the warrant for the view that the future is real (whether determined or not).

The other two combinations also seem possible: one can hold that the future is both real and determined, or that the future is not real and undetermined. My point is simply that we need to be careful not to confuse the issues surrounding the reality of the future with those surrounding the question whether the future is determined.

The other preliminary topic concerns the sceptical challenge to the possibility of omniscience. I do not plan to respond to any of the various forms of universal scepticism here, for such a topic is beyond the scope of this work. Of course, if scepticism is true, then there is no omniscient being; my topic, though, centres on the question of the possibility of a maximal knower, i.e. are there special problems that limit any possible knower in such a way that the concept of a maximal knower is incoherent? This question assumes that some knowledge is possible, and considers whether maximal knowledge is also possible. Thus, the issues raised by universal scepticism, though they have implications for the possibility of an omniscient being, are not directly relevant to the issues which concern this work. Since the work is not intended to provide a complete epistemology, I shall ignore the general issues that scepticism raises.

There is, however, a sort of scepticism which is directly relevant to this work, though it is of a much more limited variety than universal scepticism. It claims that due to the distinctive feature of human action (namely, its lack of determination by anything other than the agent himself), knowledge of actions that will be performed poses special and important problems. This topic does lie within the scope of this work, for one of the traditional problems that the doctrine of omniscience faces is that of reconciling foreknowledge with human freedom. Further scepticism about the possibility of knowledge of such actions is relevant to the purposes of this work because some philosophers have suggested that although scepticism in this area is correct, it does not undermine an adequate formulation of the doctrine of omniscience. Our consideration of this version of scepticism is not, however, an investigation of scepticism for its own sake; we will undertake consideration of it because of its connection with the proper formulation of the doctrine of omniscience. This justification for investigating this form of scepticism does not imply that we will not consider the warrant for such a version of scepticism (we shall see that the arguments for it are quite weak), it is only to say that the question of the intrinsic merits of any version of scepticism is not that which warrants discussion in this work.

The task of this chapter, then, is to determine what an omniscient being must know about the future; and, as we have seen, the issues here fall into both epistemological and metaphysical categories. Let us begin with the metaphysical view that the future is not real. I propose to examine Peter Geach's defence of this view,[1] for the discussion that will thus be generated is a perfectly general one. The considerations which, I shall suggest, undermine his view are reasons for thinking that any view which denies the reality of the future will fail. After discussing Geach's view, I shall turn to the epistemological problems surrounding knowledge of future free actions.

GEACH AND ANTI-REALISM CONCERNING THE FUTURE

The general view under consideration is that apparent knowledge of the future is only apparent, not because it is not really knowledge but because it is not really about the future – it is not *apparent knowledge* of the future (that is a claim a sceptic would make), but rather knowledge of what is only *apparently the future*. Any view of this kind must inform us as to what we are knowing about when we are knowing only the apparent future; Geach's view is that such knowledge is really only knowledge of the present tendencies of things. He says that

Future-land is a region of fairytale. 'The future' consists of certain actual trends and tendencies in the present that have not yet been fulfilled. What the Moving Finger has once writ cannot be erased: either by tears of repentance, or by the wit of man inventing a time machine, or by the very dubious piety of praying that something may or may not have happened (I have written about the last matter elsewhere). But ahead of where the Moving Finger has writ there is only blank paper; no X-ray vision can reveal what is going to stand there, any more than some scientific treatment of the paper on my desk can show what words I am going to inscribe on it.[2]

In the next chapter, I will discuss the issue of the objects of knowledge, but for now let us assume that the objects of knowledge are propositions. Geach's view about the future commits him to translating any proposition which we know and is apparently about the future into some other proposition which is not about the future. For example, it seems perfectly obvious to me that I know I will have a job next autumn. Geach is committed to denying that what I know is anything about the future; rather, he must claim, what I know is something about the present tendencies of things. I shall leave for now exactly how the translation is to proceed; the point to note, though, is that Geach's anti-realist view of the future is adequate only if such a translation can succeed.

Geach also holds an anti-deterministic view of the present tendencies of things. He claims:

> So what was going to happen at an earlier time may not be going to happen at a later time, because of some action taken in the interim. This is the way we can change the future: we can and often do bring it about that it will not be the case that p, although before our action it was going to be the case that p; it was right to say, then, 'It is going to be the case that p'. Before the operation it was right to say 'Johnny is going to bleed to death from the injury': after the operation this was no longer the case.[3]

Geach never claims that this anti-deterministic view is his reason for being an anti-realist about the future; in fact, I think he recognises that the two views are logically independent. None the less, the above quote at least presents the appearance of a confusion between anti-realism and indeterminacy about the future. This appearance results from what seems to be a conflation by Geach of the difference between a certain claim being true and it being right, or legitimate, to make that claim. Before Johnny's operation, Geach correctly notes that it was right to say 'Johnny is going to bleed to death'. However, what is not clear is that the statement *Johnny is going to bleed to death* is true before the operation. From the perspective of the observers, it appeared true and hence it was proper to claim to be true; but something can be proper to claim even though untrue. In this case we can appreciate the difference by noting that it would be appropriate for the observers to note, after the operation, that their earlier claim was false. What is true is that Johnny would have bled to death had the operation not been successful, but what would have been and what is going to be need not be the same. Conflating these two could be the result of confusing an indeterminacy view about the future with an anti-realist position about the future, for one might assume that it cannot be true that Johnny is not going to bleed to death unless it is presently determined that Johnny is not going to bleed to death.

Yet, we would be overly hasty to dismiss Geach's view so quickly, for his rejection of realism about the future does not hinge on the above example. Further, by considering his reasons for rejecting realism, we shall be in a better position to appreciate why he makes the claims he does about Johnny, his bleeding to death, and the operation that prevented his bleeding to death. These reasons can be captured by the following argument:

(1) Propositions apparently about the future are propositions about what is going to be the case.
(2) Propositions about what is going to be the case obviously refer to the present, not the future.
(3) If (1) and (2) are true, then there are no propositions about the future.
(4) If there are no propositions about the future, then the future is not real.
(5) Therefore, the future is not real.

Geach nowhere explicitly formulates this argument, but I think it captures his view. A few words are necessary in defence of its premises. (1) is apparently true in virtue of the fact that any proposition of the form *it will be that p* can be expressed as *it is going to be that p*.

(2) is a bit harder to see, but I think the idea is that sentences containing the verb phrase 'is going to be' are sentences whose verb tense is one type of present tense – namely, present progressive. Propositions expressed by present tense sentences, it might be thought, will

really be about the present tendencies of things, then, and not really about the future. So, (2) is to be accepted because present tense sentences express propositions which are about the present.

(3) is not problematic, but (4) is not quite so obvious. Geach argues that all claims about the future are propositional claims: there are no such things as future individuals or future events to which an adequate ontology must be committed. Though some may balk at this point in the argument, I shall not, for, as noted above, I am accepting the view that the reality of the future is a matter only of whether there are true propositions about what will happen. So, given that we grant Geach this ontological simplicity argument, we will have to grant (4); for on Geach's view, the existence or non-existence of the future is just the question of whether there are propositions about the future. Finally, since the above argument is valid, if we grant all the premises, we must grant that Geach has shown that the future is not real.

An initial reaction to this argument might be that the reasons given for accepting (2) seem quite weak. One might claim that there are two different senses of 'is going to be', so that (2) can be read as either:

(2a) Propositions about what is *really* going to be the case obviously refer to the present, not the future,

or

(2b) Propositions about what is going to be the case *if not prevented* obviously refer to the present, not the future.

One could then claim that, whereas (2a) is needed to make the argument valid, only (2b) is true. Hence, Geach's argument for the unreality of the future fails.

Geach considers just this objection, and his answer is that the explanation of these two different senses of 'is going to be' is circular:

> For what is prevented is always something that is going to happen, in the very sense of 'going to happen' that we are supposed to be explaining; 'prevent' has to be explained in terms of this 'going to happen', so we cannot use 'prevent' to explain it. As for the 'actually' in 'what will actually happen', it has no more logical force than a thump on the table has.[4]

Geach's response may not be perfectly clear, so I shall attempt to clarify it. In sum, the objection under consideration grants the truth of premise (1): that what is apparently about the future is about what is going to be the case. The objection arises when it is claimed that what is going to be the case only refers to the present tendencies of things, for what is going to be the case might mean what is really going to happen or what will happen if not prevented.

Geach's response is to claim that the locution, 'what is going to be the case', is fundamental in that it must be used to define the notion of prevention appealed to in (2b); hence to use the notion of prevention to describe an ambiguity in 'what is going to be the case' is circular. Since the notion of what is going to be the case must be used to define 'prevention', one can't show an ambiguity in the phrase, 'what is going to be the case', by appealing to the notion of prevention. If an ambiguity exists in 'what is going to be the case', it must be explained otherwise. And it is hard to see how a different explanation is to go.

Given the above argument (1)–(5) and Geach's response to the above objection to (2), we can explain Geach's comments about Johnny's bleeding to death which we discussed earlier. Geach claims that before the operation, Johnny was going to bleed to death; but after the operation, this was no longer the case. My worry was that this claim might be the result of confusing indeterminism about the future with anti-realism about it: one might think that it cannot be true that Johnny was not going to bleed to death unless it was presently determined that he was not. We are now in a position to see that Geach's view here does not result from such a simple confusion. Rather, he claims what he does about Johnny because he thinks that the notion of prevention cannot be explained without appeal to the notion of what is going go happen. So, when we want to clarify the notion of prevention in *the operation prevented Johnny's bleeding to death*, we must appeal to what was going to happen: Johnny was going to bleed to death until the operation was performed. Hence, Geach thinks, we are committed to the claim that before the operation Johnny was going to bleed to death. This position is much more sophisticated and at least not as clearly wrong as the simple confusion between indeterminism and anti-realism about the future.

But is Geach right that we must appeal to 'what is going to be the case' to clarify 'prevention'? Let us see if there is another way to clarify that notion. Suppose we try:

P1: The truth of p is prevented by $S =_{df.} S$ does A, and S's doing A materially implies that p is not true.

Here we have no appeal to the notion of what is going to be the case. None the less, P1 is inadequate; because, for every false proposition p, anything S does will imply that p is false. This is so since, for material conditionals, the truth of the consequent guarantees the truth of the conditional. We need to replace P1 with:

P2: The truth of p is prevented by S $=_{df.}$ S's doing A is causally sufficient, given the circumstances, for the falsity of p.

P2 is close to a correct analysis of prevention, but it is not quite adequate. For it is possible that the falsity of p is overdetermined so that even if S had not done A, p would have been false. In such a case, we should not say that S prevented the truth of p. So we must alter P2 to:

P2′: The truth of p is prevented by S $=_{df.}$ S's doing A is causally sufficient in the circumstances for the falsity of p, and the circumstances apart from S's doing A are such that p would have been true, were those circumstances to obtain.

Does P2′ appeal to the notion 'is going to be the case'? Perhaps Geach would claim it does; for the past tense of 'is going to be the case' is 'was going to be the case', and the above definition seems equivalent to the claim that what is prevented is something that was going to be the case. Thus, Geach might claim that P2′ is equivalent to:

P3: The truth of p is prevented by S $=_{df.}$ S's doing A is causally sufficient in the circumstances for the falsity of p, and p was going to be the case had S not done A.

Yet, even if P3 is equivalent to P2′, it is not clear how this equivalence aids Geach's view. The point of this discussion is to consider whether the notion of prevention can be explained without appeal to the notion of what is going to be the case. For Geach to be right that such an explanation cannot be given, it is not enough that P3 be equivalent to P2′. What Geach must defend is the claim that a set of circumstances is sufficient for the truth of p is *the same claim as* that p was going to be true; mere equivalence, even necessary equivalence, is not sufficient. Even if the claims are necessarily equivalent, it does not follow that they are identical nor does it follow that one locution is more fundamental and the other only derivative. Geach has issued a challenge to define prevention without appeal to what is going to happen; P2′ can meet the challenge even if it is necessarily equivalent to P3.

There is also good reason to think the two definitions are not identical. Since the first conjunct in both P2′ and P3 is the same, in order for P2′ to be identical to P3, the following must be true:

P4: Were the circumstances apart from S's doing A to have obtained, p would have been true $=_{df.}$ had S not done A, p was going to be true.

P4, though, is false, for the two claims involve different properties. To see this consider the following claim: if Joe had not mowed his lawn on Saturday, it would have rained on Friday. Suppose that this claim is true because Joe always mows the lawn on Saturday, except when it has rained the previous day. Even though this counterfactual is true, it need not be true that had Joe not mowed his lawn on Saturday, it was going to rain on Friday. If this latter claim were entailed by the former, such an entailment would seem to imply backward causation, and even if such causation is possible, it does not normally occur. The reason this second claim could be false, even if the first is true, is that what *was going to happen* on Friday is not affected by anything that happened on Saturday, though what *would have happened* might be (as it is in our example). Hence, regarding P4, the *definiens* can be false even though the *definiendum* is true, thereby showing that P4 is false.

If P4 is false, it follows that P3 is not identical to P2′, and hence it follows that it is possible to define 'prevention' without appeal to 'what is going to be the case'. It is important not to be misled about the nature of my argument here, for I am not arguing that P3 is not equivalent to P2′. I am granting for the sake of argument that they are equivalent, but what I am attempting to show is that they are not identical. For them to be identical, any property involved in the *definiens* of the one must be involved in the *definiens* of the other. The example about Joe mowing his lawn shows that P3 involves a property that P2′ does not (namely that of backward causation), hence even if P3 and P2′ are necessarily equivalent, they are not identical.

So, we can see that Geach is wrong in claiming that one cannot clarify the notion of prevention without appeal to the notion of what is going to happen, and hence Geach's response to the objection that he is confusing two senses of 'is going to be the case' is inadequate. Perhaps there is some other problem with that objection; if there is, I do not see it. Yet, even if there is, there is a still stronger objection to be made, an objection to Geach's joint affirmation of (1) and (2) in his argument for the unreality of the future. To see this, consider:

(8) The present tends towards p's being true, but p will in fact be false even though no one prevents p from being true.

(8) is not a self-contradiction; tendencies can exist and yet not be realised. To see this, simply consider the present tendencies of a die loaded so as to come up a six. The present state of the die is such that it tends towards the truth of the proposition *the die comes up a six* (apart from intervention or prevention). Let us suppose that there is no interference or prevention with the tendencies in question. Does it follow that the die will come up a six? Of course not. The present can tend towards a six coming up, and yet a two actually comes up. The present tendencies of the die do not guarantee that what is tended towards will occur.

Even if the present causally determined the truth of *p*, it does not follow that (8) is a contradiction; for causal determination does not entail logical determinism – the view that each state of the universe entails the next state of the universe for every such state. If there is no such entailment relation between the various states of the universe, then not even a deterministic view about the future is sufficient to show that (8) is a contradiction. In order for (8) to be a contradiction, it must be logically impossible for it to be true; and it being logically impossible requires that the first conjunct entail the falsity of the second; and only if causal determinism entails logical determinism can the causal determination in the present that *p* will be true be sufficient to make (8) a contradiction.

Further, if (8) is consistent, then either (1) or (2) is false, for the affirmation of both (1) and (2) requires that (8) is a contradiction. (1) requires that (8) be equivalent to:

(8′) The present tends towards *p*'s being true, but *p* is going to be false even though no one prevents it from being true.

In addition, (2) requires that talk of what is going to be the case is just talk about the present tendencies of things. Thus, according to (2), (8′) is equivalent to:

(8″) The present tends towards *p*'s being true, but the present does not tend toward *p*'s being true even though no one prevents it from being true.

A quick glance at (8″) shows that something has gone wrong, for (8″) is clearly a contradiction. Since (8″) is supposed to be a translation of (8), either the move required by (1) or the move required by (2) is defective. For, whereas (8) is clearly a consistent proposition, (8″) is just as clearly an inconsistent proposition. Hence, since (8) is not a self-contradiction and translating it according to the requirement of (1) and (2) generates (8″), which is a self-contradiction, Geach's argument for the unreality of the future contains a false premise.

Geach seems at one place to recognise that something like (8) is not a self-contradiction, for he says, 'I myself do not identify what does not happen with what is prevented.'⁵ Geach is surely right not to identify what does not happen with what is prevented, but if one grants that what *does* not happen is not to be identified with what is prevented, one ought also to grant that what *will* not happen is not to be identified with what is (or will be) prevented. The step from this last claim to (8) is small: if what won't happen is not what is prevented, then what will happen is not identical to what is going to happen apart from prevention, for some things will happen which go contrary to present tendencies even though no interference with those tendencies occurs. So, there is probably good reason to think that (8) is more than merely consistent. Even though its mere consistency is sufficient to show that either (1) or (2) is false, there is good reason to think that (8) is true.

This discussion has a more general application to the topic of the reality of the future than it might initially seem. For the steps that Geach's argument makes are just the sorts of steps that any denial of the reality of the future must make. It must be claimed that, whatever ontological terminology one prefers, apparent knowledge of these entities is really only knowledge of present entities. For Geach, this claim amounts to reducing propositions apparently about the future to propositions only about the present. My suggestion is that for any analogous claim with different ontological presuppositions, an alternative version of (8) can be constructed with the same decisive property of (8) – namely, not being a self-contradiction. If such an analogue can be constructed for any attempt to reduce the future to the present, no argument for the unreality of the future can succeed. I conclude then that the future is real, and that in order to be omniscient, a being must know about it.

So, an omniscient being must know about the future, but must he know all of the future in order to be omniscient? Swinburne has argued that a being cannot know all of the future and has also argued that this lack of knowledge does not undermine the claims of omniscience. He argues that the future actions of free individuals are impossible to know, and if he is right there are important implications for the doctrine of omniscience. So let us turn to Swinburne's scepticism.

SWINBURNE'S SCEPTICISM

Swinburne does not claim that there are no truths about the future, as does Geach. He claims:

> Ordinarily we speak of claims about the future (including claims about any future free actions) being true or false. I may say on Tuesday 'Jones will go to London tomorrow', and you may comment 'What you say is true'. Suppose Jones does go to London on Wednesday. Then, on Thursday, looking back, someone may say to me 'What you said on Tuesday was true'. In normal use, propositions about a named future time (including claims about any future free actions) are true or false – timelessly. We may not *know* them to be true or false, until the occurrence of that of which they speak. That which makes them true or false may also lie in the future. But what I claim may be true, even if I do not know it to be true, and even if what I claim has yet to occur.[6]

I do not want to endorse all that Swinburne has to say here about the future; all I wish to note is that any restriction Swinburne places on what an omniscient being must know in order to be omniscient cannot result in his view because of an anti-realist position about the future. The restrictions required result from purely epistemological, not metaphysical, concerns.

The restrictions Swinburne thinks apply result from his sceptical views about the possibility of knowledge of future free actions. Swinburne holds both that knowledge of future free actions is not possible and that this fact does not imply that no being can be omniscient. So, there are two distinct claims to be considered here: (i) that knowledge of future free actions is not possible, and (ii) that a being can be omniscient even though there is such a restriction on what can be known.

First, consider Swinburne's claims concerning the impossibility of knowledge of future free actions. Swinburne reasons as follows. If persons are free (I shall assume that 'free' is to be taken in line with the indeterminacy view of freedom), then they are able to do otherwise than they actually do. Now, suppose some being *B* has beliefs about what a person will do. Then the truth of *B*'s belief about that person depends on what that person chooses to do: if the person chooses to act in accord with *B*'s belief, then *B*'s belief is true; but if the person chooses to act contrary to *B*'s belief, then *B*'s belief is false. This ability to choose does not, of course, prevent any *B* from having all true beliefs about the future free actions of persons, but it does make the having of all true beliefs depend on what free creatures do or do not do. In other words, no being *B* could be omniscient unless as a matter of fact no person ever chose to make *B*'s beliefs false.

Swinburne thinks that this argument raises problems for the doctrine of omniscience. He says:

> Yet, since the free actions of men, although influenced, are not necessitated by other agents or prior states of the world, if neverthe-less all of *B*'s beliefs turned out to be true that would be a very fortunate coincidence, to say the least. Surely a theist does not want to claim that God is omniscient in this very precarious way.[7]

Swinburne's view, though, is not that we ought to give up the doctrine of omniscience. His point is that we need a better formulation of the doctrine, and he uses as precedent the way in which omnipotence has been understood in order to prevent requiring an omnipotent being to perform logically impossible tasks. Swinburne says:

> As we saw in the last chapter, theologians, such as Aquinas, have been careful to explain omnipotence, not as the ability to do anything, but (roughly) as the ability to do anything logically possible ... It would be natural to develop an account of omnis-cience along similar lines, not as knowledge of everything true, but (very roughly) as knowledge of everything true which is logically possible to know. I therefore suggest the following understanding of omniscience. A person P is omniscient at a time t if and only if he knows of every true proposition about t or an earlier time that is true and also he knows of every true proposition about a time later than t, such that what it reports is physically necessitated by some cause at t or earlier, that is true.[8]

Let us call Swinburne's view a 'limited doctrine of omniscience', and the view which he rejects (the view that omniscience requires knowledge of everything that is true) the 'traditional doctrine of omniscience'. Swinburne's claim, then, is that the limited doctrine is able to preserve both the freedom of human actions and the omniscience of God. God is still omniscient even though he does not know what free creatures will do, for such knowledge is not possible, in Swinburne's view.

Essential to this view is the claim that knowledge of what free creatures will do is *impossible*. If such knowledge were possible, but not actual, Swinburne would be forced to give up his view that there is an omniscient being. Hence, one question we must ask is whether there is any good reason for thinking that such knowledge is impossible.

Given that Swinburne has granted that true beliefs about the future are possible, he must maintain that it is the justification condition for knowledge which cannot be satisfied.[9] The relevant claim from the argument above would seem to be that a being who had all true beliefs about future free actions would be quite lucky, and there are two ways one might take this claim to affect the justification for the beliefs in question. First, he might mean that the element of luck would infect any belief about what a free individual will do. Alternatively, one might think that the problem of luck only affects a maximal set of such beliefs, so that, even though some of the members may be epistemically secure enough to be justified, the entire set is not secure enough for all the members to be justified.

However, to make sense of Swinburne's move to the limited doctrine which he defends, we must interpret him in the first sense. For if Swinburne grants that some individual beliefs can be epistemically secure enough to be justifiably held, it is doubtful that he can maintain that it is impossible to know what a free individual will know. Yet, his limited doctrine of omniscience requires that such knowledge be impossible.

My point here is not that there are no problems in defending that a being can know the complete course of future free behaviour. Rather, my point is that Swinburne intends the emphasis on luck to motivate the move from the traditional to his limited doctrine of omniscience, he must defend that the luck in question infects every possible belief about any possible free action; it is not sufficient for his purposes to show that the whole collection of such beliefs cannot be justifiably held. For if the latter point is the only one that holds, we do not get Swinburne's construal of omniscience. So let us concentrate on the issue of whether any true belief about a future free action can be justified.

There are three ways one could defend that justified beliefs are not possible regarding future free actions. The first is to affirm an infallibilist conception of justification: to hold that one is not justified in believing p unless one's evidence for p guarantees the truth of p. Then the worry Swinburne has about the fortuitousness of having all true beliefs about the future would make sense, for if believing all and only truths about the future would be a fortuitous coincidence at best, God could not have the sort of evidence that guarantees the truth of what he believes. If the evidence did guarantee truth, the fortuitousness charge would be obviously unfounded.

Yet this attempted defence of his limited doctrine is not especially promising, for our ordinary concept of justification is not infallibilistic. We have all sorts of justified beliefs about the past, the future, the existence of the external world and other minds even though we are capable of error in all of these areas. Surely affirming an infallibilistic conception of justification is simply a mistake.

None the less, we are inclined to think that God must be incapable of error, and this inclination leads to another possible approach to claiming that at least God cannot know what free individuals will do. One might reason as follows. In order for a being to be God, he must not only know everything there is to know, but He must also be incapable of not knowing what there is to be known. In other words, He must be essentially omniscient, not just omniscient. No matter how this world might turn out, in order to be God, He would have to know everything, i.e. God's knowledge of the future cannot contingently depend on the world turning out one particular way rather than another. But, if actions are really free, knowledge of those actions could only be contingent, i.e. it would not be possible for a being to have the sort of knowledge which precludes the possibility of mistake. Thus, no being could be essentially omniscient about free actions, for if actions are free, then their being known depends on the person in question not making the belief in question false; and if the knowledge in question is contingent in this fashion, then the world might have turned out so that the being we call 'God' would not have been omniscient. But, then, we ought not to understand omniscience to require knowledge of free actions. For, if knowledge of free actions is required, so is essential knowledge of free actions – and the latter is clearly not possible. Hence, to be omniscient, a being cannot be required to know what free actions any individual will perform.

There are hints in Swinburne's work that something like one of these arguments lies behind his acceptance of the limited doctrine of omniscience, for he frequently points out that no one can know *for sure* what a free creature will do. One would not worry about such lack of infallibility unless one either thought that justification requires infallibility, or one had special reasons for requiring infallibility of any being worthy of the title 'God'. The first option we have already rejected, so let us consider the second option, i.e. let us suppose that no being is worthy of the title 'God' unless that being is infallible. One could then argue as above: if we defend the doctrine of omniscience in accord with the traditional formulation, then we preserve omniscience at the expense of infallibility. Though infallibility is lost given only the doctrine of omniscience, it follows from the doctrine of essential omniscience and, given the contingency of knowledge of future free actions, essential omniscience is not possible. The solution to this difficulty might then be to claim that since infallibility is not possible about the future, perhaps God would be kind enough to preserve our philosophical theory about Him by just not holding any beliefs at all about the future, except for those parts of the future about which He cannot be wrong. Perhaps we could thus preserve both the infallibility intuitions and the doctrine of omniscience at the same time.

Just in the stating of the view, one can easily see that it ought to be dismissed quickly. God could not be kind enough to preserve our theorising unless it was impossible for Him to hold beliefs about the future free actions of individuals, for to be infallible a being must not only have true beliefs but must also be such that whatever sort of belief he might form would be true. Thus, even if God refused to form beliefs about the future, that would not preserve the infallibility intuition; in order for that intuition to be preserved, it must be impossible for God to form beliefs about the future. Hence, we cannot preserve both infallibility and omniscience in the way just posited.

Further, we should not be enticed to alter the doctrine of omniscience simply because, on that understanding, God could not be essentially omniscient. One should not require a being to have any property essentially in order to be God unless it is possible to have that property essentially. And even worse, one clearly should not infer that some property cannot be instantiated at all simply because it cannot be essentially instantiated. Hence, whether it is infallibility *via* essential omniscience, or just essential omniscience alone that is appealed to in the above argument, there is not much to be said for the argument.

There is also a quite severe paradox generated if this line of reasoning is allowed. Since human knowledge does not require infallibility, humans can know what some of the future free actions will be. God cannot, since his knowledge requires infallibility. Thus, an individual can be God and hence omniscient on Swinburne's view even if that individual knows less about a particular domain than mere humans. Such an implication is surely too adverse to sensibility to detain us even for a moment.

Thus, in order to defend that an individual is essentially omniscient, one must begin by describing how he is omniscient. One cannot start by requiring essential omniscience, and then concluding that because something cannot be known in every possible world that it need not be known in this world. To do so results in a doctrine of omniscience that allows a being to be omniscient though that being knows quite a bit less than we do.

There is a third and final way that I can think of to defend the claim that that God need not know what free individuals will do in order to be omniscient. One might argue that future free actions have characteristics which prevent any individual from knowing that they will occur. Swinburne seems to suggest that this is so, at least if the being in question is a perfectly free one. First, Swinburne claims to doubt that any person could be justified in all their beliefs about the future free actions of humans. He considers the reply that humans are not perfectly free in the sense that their choices are influenced, though not necessitated, by external factors. Given these influences, perhaps prediction is possible. But, when the agent is a perfectly free one, matters are quite different. Swinburne says:

> If P is to be justified in supposing that his beliefs about A's actions are true, he must be justified in believing that there are correlations between P's beliefs about them and A's future actions. But given that nothing in the past in any way influences what A does (and P knows this), P could only be justified in supposing that there was a correlation between his beliefs and P's actions if he were justified in supposing that P's actions made a difference to his belief; that his beliefs about them were caused (or largely influenced by) P's actions. But to make this supposition is to allow backward causation, which as I have suggested, is apparently something logically impossible. Hence I conclude that P could not be justified in holding beliefs about the future actions of a perfectly free agent.[10]

Earlier, Swinburne had claimed that a perfectly free individual is an individual 'not influenced in his choices by any causal factors'.[11] So, Swinburne's claim is that justified beliefs about the future actions of such a perfectly free individual is impossible.

If sound, this argument does give some reason to give up the traditional construal of omniscience and accept Swinburne's limited doctrine in its place. For, even if it is impossible to know what a perfectly free individual will do, it is none the less now true that that individual will perform a certain action (if he really will). Thus, if being omniscient requires knowing all truths, no being could be omniscient. Yet, since it is not possible, if Swinburne is right, to know what a perfectly free individual will do, this is not a mark against the intellectual excellence of anyone. Hence, knowing what such an individual will do is not required for omniscience as it is not possible to know this.

On the other hand, we do not get Swinburne's formulation of the doctrine of omniscience from the preceding argument. Above I formulated a limited doctrine as follows: a being is omniscient if and only if that being knows all that can be known. Swinburne formulates the doctrine using the notion of physical necessitation – an omniscient being only needs to know all that is or has occurred, and all about the future that is physically necessitated by the past or present. This difference between the two formulations is important because, in the above argument, Swinburne does not claim to show that imperfectly free actions cannot be foreknown, he only argues that perfectly free actions cannot. So, if there are imperfectly free actions, Swinburne's account implies that they need not be foreknown; the formulation I gave above (that omniscience requires knowing all that can be known) does not imply that they need not be foreknown unless we can find some argument to show that they cannot be foreknown. Swinburne needs to argue more than just that perfectly free actions cannot be foreknown; he must also show that imperfectly free ones cannot be foreknown either.

Thus, even if we grant Swinburne that omniscience only requires knowing all that can be known and that perfectly free actions cannot be foreknown we cannot accept his account of omniscience unless we also grant that imperfectly free actions cannot be foreknown. Swinburne thinks there is something doubtful about claiming that all beliefs about imperfectly free actions can be justified. Yet, as we have seen, he does not give any good reason for thinking that this is so. Further, there do not seem to be any reasons apart from what he explicitly states that could support such a sceptical view about knowledge of future free actions. Hence, we ought to reject at least Swinburne's limited doctrine of omniscience. If our characterisation of omniscience must not be the traditional one, the limitations that result from Swinburne's considerations can at best apply to future perfectly free actions.

But has Swinburne even shown that future, perfectly free actions cannot be known? What I wish to argue is that if God can know what imperfectly free actions will be done, he can know what actions he will do. And, since all God's actions are perfectly free, knowing what imperfectly free actions will be done implies knowing that at least some perfectly free actions will be done. The argument for this is rather simple. Suppose God knows in 1920 that Hitler will murder 6 000 000 Jews by 1945 unless He or other free agents intervene to stop him. Since we are assuming that God can know what imperfectly free actions will be done, and since we are assuming that human actions are all imperfectly free at best, God can know that no one but He will intervene. God is then faced with an alternative. Either He will intervene and stop Hitler or He will not. Since God is perfectly free, either course will be perfectly free. If we assume with Swinburne that a perfectly free agent always and only acts on what there is an overriding reason to act on,[12] it follows that if God does not know which course He will follow, it is because he does not know that there is an overriding reason to act on. However, either He is not omniscient on other grounds (He lacks insight, for example, into what there are overriding reasons for), or there really are no overriding reasons in this case. Therefore, it at least follows that if there is no other objection to the doctrine of omniscience, and if there are overriding reasons for a certain course of action, God will do that action.

Further, suppose that there are no overriding reasons for either course of action. Still God can consider what decisions he will make in such a situation, and know that if He were in such and such a situation He would choose to do so and so. There is much more to say about this sort of conditional, which some have called counterfactuals of freedom, but for now I wish only to point out that Swinburne does not offer any objections to the view that there are counterfactuals which are true and yet are about the free actions of individuals. Indeed, if there are such truths and God could know them, then even the actions of a perfectly free agent can be foreknown.

The only hope of escape from this argument, other than denying that there are counterfactuals of the relevant sort, is to claim that God's evaluation of the reasons for acting and His acting occur instantaneously, so that God cannot consider beforehand what He will do. But there will be many cases in which this is not true. There will be cases in which God has an overriding reason to allow a certain human action to occur, and His allowing this action gives Him an overriding reason for intervening in human history in the future. Presumably, the fall of Adam and God's ultimate purpose in Christ fit this pattern. God surely can have an overriding reason at *t* for doing action *A* later than *t*. And thus, God can know what He will do in the future by knowing what overriding reasons there are and will be.

What is left open for Swinburne is to argue that imperfectly free actions cannot be foreknown. Yet he does not see how to argue for this view, or it is likely that he would have given such an argument. Further, it is clear that a very strong argument is necessary here, for it appears quite obvious that each of us knows quite a bit about our own future actions and the future actions of those around us.

Earlier we saw that a defence of Swinburne's view of omniscience required two steps. First, the sceptical conclusion he draws would need defence; and secondly, the compatibility of this scepticism with there being an omniscient being would have to be defended. Our discussion to this point has shown that the first step of his defence is, at best, weak.

There is an even stronger conclusion to draw, however, and it is that there is no good reason for thinking that the second step could be defended either. The fundamental intuition in Swinburne's account is that an omniscient being need only know all that can be known, rather than all that is true. Swinburne's argument for this claim comes from explications of the doctrine of omnipotence, where theologians have been careful to say that an omnipotent being need only be able to perform any logically possible task. Even if Swinburne's limited doctrine is inadequate, as I have argued, there still remains a fundamental break between limited construals of omniscience and the traditional construal, for even if Swinburne is wrong about which propositions cannot be known, it may still be possible that some cannot be known. Hence, a defender of a limited account might query, shouldn't we still prefer a limited account to a traditional one because of the analogy with the doctrines of omnipotence?

The answer is no, for there is a significant difference between the statement of the omnipotence doctrine and limited construals of omniscience. The analogy intended to support a limited doctrine of omniscience is between feasible tasks and knowable truths and between unfeasible tasks and unknowable truths; but the analogy is crucially defective. Whereas an unknowable truth is still a truth, an unfeasible task is not a task at all. When one asks that a being B do an act falling under description D, where D is self-contradictory, the proper response is that there is no such act at all. (A good analogy here is the response one might make to a child who claimed to be drawing a square circle. We might say, 'You may be drawing something, but it is not a square circle, for there aren't and can't be any such things.' It is not that there is or could be a thing (an impossible object) which has a certain property (being impossible) which prevents the child from drawing it – then we should have said, 'You can't draw those sorts of things.' The point is rather that there literally are no such things, nor could there be.) Yet, in the domain of knowledge, an unknowable truth is still a truth.

Perhaps a bit more precision would allow the disanalogy to become more apparent. Both in the domain of power and in the domain of knowledge, there is a distinction between the person who either knows or does something and that which that person knows or does; a distinction between person and the thing done. In the domain of power, we have the doer and the task; in the domain of knowledge, we have the knower and the proposition known. When, in the domain of power, there is an apparent limitation on what can be done, it is a limitation regarding the thing done: self-contradictory descriptions are not descriptions of any task at all. On the other hand, in the domain of knowledge, the apparent limitation regards the *person* in question: the knower is somehow unable to access the proposition in question. A proper analogy between omnipotence and omniscience would countenance limitations on the same side.

Of significance here is that the traditional construal of omniscience involves just such a feature. One might insist that an omniscient being knows all propositions. That is impossible, since not all propositions are true. Hence, there is an apparent limitation involved in the traditional doctrine of omniscience, just as there is an apparent limitation in the doctrine of omnipotence. An omnipotent being need not be able to perform impossible tasks and an omniscient being need not know false propositions.

Thus the analogy intended to support limited construals of omniscience actually supports the traditional construal instead, for it is only on the traditional construal of omniscience that the analogy with omnipotence holds. To speak of limitations here is, of course, a misnomer: impossible tasks are not among the things to be done, and false propositions are not among the things to be known.

On the other hand, the limitations in a limited doctrine of omniscience are real limitations. In such a view, there can be all sorts of truths which, though unknown, do not cast doubt on the doctrine of omniscience. Such a construal could imply that everyone is omniscient, if a radical scepticism were true (one which implied that nothing could be known except one's own existence and mental states). If all that could be known are the contents of one's own mind, and if it is true that one cannot be mistaken about the contents of one's mind, a limited account of omniscience would seem to imply that every one of us is omniscient. (Note that I am not claiming either that this version of scepticism is true or that we cannot be mistaken about the contents of our minds – my objection here rests only on the fact that we have no guarantee that such views are wrong.) If these views were true, the conclusion to draw is that everyone is even more removed from the state of being omniscient that we presently think. To call such beings omniscient would clearly be a misnomer, for the limitations of such beings are too real to be dismissed in the way that logically impossible tasks can be dismissed in discussing omnipotence. The point is that the limitations allowed by a limited construal of omniscience are real precisely because the limitations are imposed on the *person* component of knowledge, not regarding what is known.

The conclusion to be drawn then is that a limited doctrine of omniscience, which claims that an omniscient being is one who knows all that can be known, should be rejected in favour of the traditional construal, one which (roughly) claims that an omniscient being is one who knows everything that is true. The specific limited doctrine proposed by Swinburne is inadequate, and, more generally, the analogy with the doctrine of omnipotence intended to support the claim that some sort of limited doctrine should be accepted really only supports the traditional doctrine of omniscience. Hence, there is good reason to accept the traditional construal and good reason to reject any limited construal.

CONCLUSION

I have not attempted in this chapter to show that God can know the future. All I have tried to do is to show that unless a being does know the future, that being cannot be omniscient. In order to defend this view, I examined two attempts to deny the claim. The first was a purely metaphysical claim; the claim that since the future is not real, it cannot be known. I suggested that no argument of this sort could work because the apparent futurity of the objects of our intentional attitudes cannot be eliminated.

The second attempt to deny my claim was an epistemological attempt; in particular, a version of limited scepticism about the future. This scepticism is directed at showing not that there is no omniscient being, but rather that we need a new understanding of omniscience – a limited version of the doctrine. I argued that Swinburne's particular limitations are inadequate. More importantly though, I suggested that the reasons given for accepting any limited version of the doctrine are actually reasons for accepting the traditional doctrine of omniscience.

For the limitations imposed by the traditional doctrine (that a being need not know false propositions to be omniscient) are only apparent limitations of the being in question, whereas the limitations imposed by limited versions of the doctrine (where a being need not know all truths, but only all truths that can be known) are real limitations on the knowledge of the being in question. The conclusion to be drawn is that a being must know all truths in order to be omniscient, and that includes knowing truths about the future and in particular about the future free actions of persons.

2 Knowledge and its Objects

INTRODUCTION

The last chapter assumed that the objects of knowledge are propositions. This assumption requires defence and part of this chapter will be devoted to this. In addition, we must discuss the nature of knowledge in order to be clear about the requirements of omniscience, and therefore this chapter will investigate the nature of knowledge and its objects. This statement of purpose is, of course, a little overstated; for certainly a complete epistemology cannot be presented in one chapter. Rather, I shall investigate the nature of knowledge in so far as it bears on the doctrine of omniscience. First, I shall discuss the nature of knowledge in sufficient detail to develop a preliminary understanding of the claim that there is an omniscient being, and I shall also distinguish that claim from the claim that there is a being who has the property of being omniscient essentially.

A greater portion of the chapter, though, will be devoted to the issues that surround the topic of the objects of knowledge. When one knows something, two things are true. First, one's mind is in a certain intentional state, which I shall assume is the state of believing. There are other intentional states that one's mind could be in, such as wishing, hoping, desiring, or intending; but none of these states is the sort of state that is involved in knowing something. There are theories of knowledge on which knowledge and belief are distinct mental states, and a complete epistemology ought to consider such views. Here such views can be ignored, for my intention is to defend what I have called the traditional construal of omniscience, and the standard construal of knowledge requires belief as one of the conditions for knowledge. This standard construal of knowledge can be found as early as Plato's *Theaetetus*, and is clearly the accepted view among contemporary epistemologists. Though none of this amounts to a defence that belief is necessary for knowledge, it does justify ignoring the issue in a work like this not devoted to purely epistemological concerns. So, our first point is that there is a mental state involved in knowing – namely believing.

Second, in addition to being in the mental state of belief when one knows something, the particular intentional state one is in is directed towards something – when one is in the state of believing, one believes something. The issue of the objects of knowledge, or of intentional attitudes in general, is just the issue of what this something is.

Initially, it may seem that the proper response is that there are all sorts of things which are the objects of intentional attitudes: we wish for happiness, remember the defeat of Germany in the Second World War, intend to win, believe in God, know of the perils of hitch-hiking. So perhaps the objects include states of affairs, events, actions, persons, and even possibilities.

Yet it would certainly be a virtue of a philosophical theory to reduce the apparent multiplicity here, and there is just such a reductionist view that we shall begin by considering. In that view, contrary to the appearances above, there is really only one object of all intentional attitudes. Intentional attitudes are those directed towards propositions, and the traditional account of omniscience in which an omniscient being is one who knows all true propositions, fits naturally with the propositional theory of the objects of intentional attitudes. So, in discussing the nature and definition of the kind of knowledge that omniscience includes, the discussion will turn to an explication of the propositional view about the objects of intentional attitudes.

In spite of its noteworthy successes in unifying the account to be given of intentional attitudes, the propositional view faces serious objections. I shall discuss some of these problems and some of the suggestions for solving these problems. I shall argue that the extant solutions are inadequate; but that, with perhaps some substantive revisions in the propositional view, the problems with the propositional theory of the objects of intentional attitudes need not undermine the traditional doctrine of omniscience.

Our first task, then, is to formulate and examine the traditional account of omniscience. In so doing, we shall see that the traditional account at least originates in a propositional theory concerning the objects of belief and knowledge, thus leading us to the topic of the objects of knowledge. Let us first clarify the traditional account.

THE TRADITIONAL CONCEPTION OF OMNISCIENCE

What we are calling the traditional account of omniscience is this: what it means for a being to be omniscient is for that being to be such that, for all propositions *p*, *p* is true if and only if that being knows that p. As Geach puts it, ' ''God knows that p' is true if and only if the plain 'p' is true. And whenever it makes sense to ask whether, or who, or why, then we may assert that God knows whether, or who, or why.'[1]

There are two key notions in the brief statement of the view above. One is that a certain proposition is true, the other is that of knowing that a proposition is true. I shall ignore the philosophical issues surrounding truth here. The conception of truth that I shall be using is what I take to be our ordinary understanding of the term: whether a proposition is true or not is determined by whether it reflects the way the world is or not. I shall not try to state what this metaphorical use of 'reflects' comes to, but some simple examples will help clarify what I mean. It is true that snow is white. Why? Because that proposition, the proposition that snow is white, bears an intimate connection with the way the world is, for the world is structured in such a way that snow really is white. Likewise, it is true that horses have four legs because the world is such that horses have four legs.

The other notion in the preceding statement of the doctrine of omniscience is the notion of knowledge. Philosophers have long recognised that to know that a claim is true requires that the claim be true and that one believe that it is true. It has also been recognised that these two conditions (belief and truth) are not sufficient for knowledge, for one can have a true belief in much the same way as a person might make a lucky guess: one may happen to hold a belief and, by sheer luck, that belief may be true. Since knowledge is incompatible with this sort of luck, some other condition is necessary beyond mere true belief in order to have knowledge. In addition to true belief, the belief must be grounded or justified in such a way that it is not just sheer luck that what one believes is true. Hence, knowledge requires justified true belief (at least).

A word is in order at this point about recent theories of knowledge which deny that justification is a necessary condition for knowledge. Theories of a causal sort are generally given to making such claims.[2] I have two responses to such claims. First, theories of knowledge which deny that justification is necessary for knowledge are normally motivated by attempts to provide an epistemology compatible with a materialistic conception of the world.[3] Obviously, a theist will not and need not be moved by such considerations. A theist need not clarify his position on omniscience so that it does not beg the question against materialist conceptions of the universe – after all, his merely being a theist is sufficient to violate that conception. If a materialist has any interest in clarifying what it is for a being to be omniscient, let him worry about how to clarify it in such a way that it does not violate materialist constraints. Our interest in omniscience is from a view already incompatible with materialism; even if we were to delete certain elements incompatible with materialism, the resultant theory would be no more appealing to the materialist than it presently is.

Second, and more important, I am not construing the term 'justifica-tion' so that it entails any substantive commitments about the nature of justification. What is meant by saying that justifiction is necessary for knowledge is explained in the way I introduced the requirement above: it is merely some condition necessary in addition to true belief which accounts for the fact that lucky guesses are not knowledge. Hence, there is nothing in my introduction of a justification condition for knowledge that makes this claim incompatible with the claims of those who deny that justification is necessary for knowledge, for they too agree that knowledge requires more than true belief. Hence, we need not worry about those positions which claim that justification is not necessary for knowledge.

There is, however, one issue about the nature of justification which we cannot ignore, for in attempting to understand what it is for an omniscient being to have a justification for his true beliefs, we face a crossroads: do we clarify what it is like for our beliefs to be justified, or for God's beliefs to be justified? If we begin with the nature of God's justification, we would begin by noting that God cannot be mistaken about anything He believes. Proceeding in this fashion, we would require that an omniscient being be incapable of error concerning anything which he believes.

Such a procedure would be a mistake, though, for this procedure tends to confuse the doctrine of omniscience with the doctrine of essential omniscience. To say that a being has a certain property essentially is to say that that being would have that property regardless of how the world turned out; thus to say that God is essentially omniscient implies that He would know everything no matter how the world turned out, and thus that He couldn't make a mistake in His beliefs. So, being essentially omniscient implies an incapacity for error.

Our first task is to clarify the doctrine of omniscience, and since beginning with the nature of God's justification can generate a confu-sion between omniscience and essential omniscience, we ought to begin elsewhere – by clarifying what sort of justification any sort of know-ledge requires, and then clarify the doctrine of omniscience using that conception. To begin, then, let us ask what sort of justification knowledge requires.

To many in the history of philosophy, it has appeared that the justification which knowledge requires is the kind described above concerning God's knowledge; that knowledge requires a justification which eliminates the possibility of error. Though infallibilism was rejected in the previous chapter, there is an intuition behind this view which ought to be addressed: namely, that if one knows something, one cannot have made a mistake about it. This intuition is, I take it, true; the issue which needs to be addressed is whether this intuition confirms that an infallibilist conception of justification is correct. In order to achieve a proper understanding of the distinction between omniscience and essential omniscience we must first show that one can accept the above intuition, without committing oneself to a view of justification that requires the sort of impossibility of error proper only to the doctrine of essential omniscience.

The argument that the above intuition does not show that infallibilism is correct is simple, though some of the technical apparatus we need to see the force of the argument will complicate the matter a little. The reason the institution above does not commit one to infallibilism is that it is ambiguous between several different readings. The claim in question is:

(1) If S knows that p, then S cannot be mistaken about p.

One way to understand (1) is:

(2) Necessarily, (if S knows that p, then S is not mistaken about p)

Another reading is:

(3) If S knows that p, then necessarily S is not mistaken about p.

The difference between (2) and (3) reflects the ambiguity of the scope of the modal operator (in its occurrence in 'cannot') in (1). But there is still another reading of (1), for some would claim that when S knows that p, there is something about S himself or the state he is in that prohibits mistakes. In other words, some would claim that (1) should be read as ascribing a certain sort of essential property to S or some state of S.

There are two general ways to transcribe (1) along these lines, with each general way being subject to two construals depending on whether it is the person's knowledge or the person himself who has the essential property in question. The first two readings are:

(4a) If *S* knows that p, then *S* has a certain property necessarily or essentially: namely, having evidence which is such that anyone's having that evidence would obtain only if *p* were true.

(4b) If *S* knows that p, then the mental state of belief which constitutes *S*'s knowledge has the following property: it is essentially such that the evidence for *p* (the content of the mental state) obtains only if *p* is true.

The other two readings are:

(5a) For all *S*, *S* has a certain property essentially: namely, having evidence which is such that anyone's having that evidence would obtain only if *p* were true, when *S* knows that p.

(5b) For every mental state *M* of belief that p, *M* has the following property essentially: having evidence for *p* only if *p* is true, when *M* is a mental state which is knowledge.

In order to evaluate which of (2) through (5b) is the proper way to read (1), we need some information about how to understand necessity claims. The primary differences between (2)–(3) and (4a–b)–(5a–b) is that the first pair are *de dicto* necessity claims while the latter pairs are *de re* necessity claims. A *de dicto* claim *necessarily p* is true just in case *p* is true in every possible world. Alternatively, a *de re* claim *object O has property P necessarily* is true when and only when *O* has *P* in every possible world in which *O* exists.

These definitions leave unspecified how one is to conceive possible worlds. I shall take a possible world as a maximally conjunctive, yet consistent proposition. A conjunctive proposition is maximal just in case, for every proposition *p*, either *p* or *not-p* is one of the conjuncts of the conjunctive proposition. A proposition is consistent if and only if it fails to entail any contradiction.

Although under some conditions the two types of necessity claims are identical, the definitions above properly imply that the two are not generally identical. It is a necessary truth that whatever is sitting, is sitting; it is far from true that whatever is sitting, has the property of sitting necessarily. There are many ways of committing suicide, but leaving one's chair is typically not one of them.

We are now in a position to evaluate the different readings of the claim that whenever someone knows something, they cannot be mistaken. (3) above is clearly false: it claims that if *S* knows that p, then a certain proposition is necessarily true: that *S* is not mistaken about *p*. However, no proposition is true in a world unless the subject of that proposition exists in that world. Thus, the proposition that S is not mistaken about p cannot be a necessary truth unless S is a necessary being. So, if (3) is true, S must be a necessary being; yet, clearly, some of us know some things even though none of us (humans) are necessary beings. Hence, (3) is false.

Both readings (4a) and (4b) are equally problematic, for both claim that having knowledge implies that one cannot exist and lack the evidence which one has for the claim in question. This implication shows that both readings are false as well, for we can lose our knowledge without ceasing to be, and that is just what these readings deny. Forgetting what we used to know is sometimes a sad thing, but never near so sad as doing something that ends one's existence.

We are left then with (2) and (5a–b) as possible readings of (1). Both readings (5a) and (5b), it seems to me, are false as well. I know that my parents love me, even though none of my evidence for that belief is strong enough to rule out the possibility of my being mistaken. Of course, if I am mistaken, I do not know that they love me – that is just what (2) states. (2) states the truth that one cannot know something unless it is true; (5a) make the implausible claim that no evidence is good enough unless it infallibly signals the truth. Thus, I am claiming that (2), the *de dicto* necessity claim, is the only correct reading of (1); I am claiming that, though knowledge rules out the possibility of error in one sense (in the sense that one cannot know what is false), it does not rule it out in any sense which implies the infallibilism of either (5a) or (5b).

This rejection of infallibilism is not meant to be taken as a claim that God's knowledge is such as to allow that He might be mistaken. We must distinguish the nature of knowledge in itself from its instantiation in some individual. Though knowledge may not require infallibility, it may be that some knowers are infallible; it is just that our account of omniscience should not require that an omniscient being is infallible unless the nature of knowledge itself requires this. It is true that God is not only omniscient, He would be omniscient no matter how the world might turn out (or so I shall contend); yet we should not require that a being be essentially omniscient in order to be omniscient. It may turn out that the one and only possible omniscient being is essentially omniscience, and further that it is impossible that one be omniscient without being essentially omniscient. But this would be true in virtue of the nature of the omniscient being, not in virtue of omniscience itself.

So far, then, we have determined that knowledge requires justified, true belief, and that the sort of justification in question need not eliminate the possibility of error. We might then clarify the doctrine of omniscience by claiming that a being is omniscient if and only if that being believes everything that is true and is justified in believing everything that is true.

One problem with this formulation is that the phrase 'justified in believing' is ambiguous. It might mean 'has a justification for believing' or it might mean 'justifiably believes'. The difference here is critical, for a person can have a justification for believing that p and yet not justifiably believe that p because he does not hold the belief in question on the basis of, or because of, the justification for it. For example, a person might have all sorts of good reasons for thinking that the moon is not made of green cheese and yet come to accept that claim because his favourite fortune-teller says it is true. Though he has a justification for the claim in question, he does not justifiably believe that claim, for he accepts it for the wrong reasons. Hence, we must clarify the understanding above by claiming:

O: A being *B* is omniscient = $_{df.}$ *B* justifiably believes that p if and only if *p* is true.

O is the account of omniscience that I wish to defend in this work; further, it allows us to hold that the doctrine of omniscience does not require a being to have a kind of knowledge (a sort requiring infallible justification) radically different from our knowledge. On the other hand, it should be noted that O does not require that any omniscient being has knowledge which differs from ours only in extent and not in kind. For on plausible assumptions, we can show that if God is the only omniscient being, then the only omniscient being has knowledge different in kind from our own. To see this, note first that if we accept O, we can clarify essential omniscience as:

EO: Being *B* is essentially omniscient = $_{df.}$ *B* has the essential property of justifiably believing that p if and only if *p* is true.

Further, if a being is essentially omniscient, then, if that being were to believe *p*, *p* would be true; and, if *p* were to turn out to be false, that being would believe that *p* is false as well. But, consider the following understanding of absolute certainty:

AC: *p* is absolutely certain for *B* = $_{df.}$ *p* is true; *B* would believe that p only if the proposition that p were true; and *B* would fail to believe that p only if the proposition that p were not true.

Given that there could not be an omniscient being other than God and given that no being could be God unless both omniscient and essentially omniscient, it follows that no being could be omniscient without having a kind of knowledge that is quite different from our knowledge. Our knowledge is characterised by a sort of justification compatible with the possibility of error, whereas no omniscient being's knowledge can be of that sort – for if a being is omniscient, there is a cogent line of argument to show that that being must be absolutely certain of everything he knows. Thus, even though the doctrine of omniscience does not require a kind of knowledge different from our own, it might be necessary that a being has a different kind of knowledge from ours if that being is to be omniscient.

Nonetheless, even if it is impossible that there be an omniscient being whose knowledge is of the same kind as ours, that is not a sufficient reason for clarifying the doctrine of omniscience so that it requires knowledge of a different kind. Thus, there is no reason on these grounds to object to O. Rather, the fact that O is distinct from EO, i.e. the fact that omniscience defined by O is a property distinct from essential omniscience as defined by EO, is a mark in favour of O; for it is a general truth that having a property and having it essentially are different.

There is one objection I can think of to the claim that omniscience and essential omniscience are distinct. The argument for this objection is as follows. If *B* is omniscient, he not only knows what events occur in this world, he also knows what is possible and what is impossible. Thus, he knows of every maximally conjunctive and consistent proposition that it is maximally conjunctive and consistent. But, that is just to know all there is to know about every possible world; and isn't that what it is to be essentially omniscient?

No. The concept of a being knowing what every world would be like from the vantage point of a particular world (the actual one) and the concept of being such that one would know what every world would be like no matter which world were actual, are distinct concepts. The first concept has explicit reference only to the actual world; the second does not preclude the actuality of any world. Hence, omniscience is not identical to essential omniscience.

As I claimed above before investigating the distinction between omniscience and essential omniscience, O is the account of omniscience which I shall defend. In this particular chapter, I wish to defend that O's assumption that omniscience can be defined in terms of propositional knowledge, and that O's implications for the nature of knowledge are not problematic. Thus, there are two sorts of objections which we must examine in this chapter, the first bearing on the account of knowledge O seems to imply and the second on that account's assumption that the objects of knowledge are propositions.

OBJECTIONS TO O

It might be thought that some recent work in epistemology shows that O is an inadequate construal of omniscience. For, as Gettier has shown, it is possible to have a justified true belief which is not an instance of knowledge.[4] Consider a rather simple case. Jones has told Smith that he (Jones) owns a Ford. Jones has given Smith as much evidence as one could ask for to make it reasonable for Smith to believe that Jones owns a Ford: Jones has driven a Ford to Smith's home, shown him a title to it, etc. Thus, Smith's belief that Jones owns a Ford is fully justified by the evidence Smith has for that belief. The example temporally begins in Smith's office, where Smith, Jones, and the janitor are. Smith reasons that, since Jones is in the office and owns a Ford, there is someone in his office who owns a Ford. This belief is as reasonable as his earlier one that Jones owns a Ford. None the less, the earlier belief is false: Jones has deceived Smith and really owns no car at all. However, as it turns out, Smith's belief that someone in his office owns a Ford is true; for, contrary to what Smith knows, the janitor owns a Ford. Smith thereby has a justified true belief that someone in his office owns a Ford, but he does not know that someone in his office owns a Ford. His justification for that belief is defective in a certain way, a way which prevents him from having knowledge.

Recently, Grim has argued on these grounds that O is an inadequate clarification of the doctrine of omniscience. He claims:

> An omniscient being in the sense of O cannot hold false beliefs, and moreover cannot hold beliefs from mere caprice or without justification. If justified true belief were knowledge, O would be the answer to our difficulties. But of course knowledge is not merely justified true belief. What O leaves open then, is the uncomfortable possibility that God, although justified in believing all and only true propositions, does not know them – just as the individuals of Gettier's examples, although justified in believing certain propositions, cannot be said to know them.[5]

What I wish to argue is that such cases do not cast doubt on the adequacy of O. Central to the Gettier cases is a certain sort of limitation regarding that of which the person in question is aware. In the earlier case, Smith does not believe that the janitor owns a Ford. Further, he is not aware that Jones has been deceiving him. Now, none of these limitations occur for any being omniscient by O. Such a being would justifiably believe that the janitor owns a Ford, and thereby would have a justified belief that someone in the office owns a Ford. Further, by O, an omniscient being would not justifiably believe that Jones owns a Ford, for it is false that Jones owns a Ford – and, by O, no omniscient being believes anything which is false. So, Gettier-like cases do not seem to raise any difficulty for O.

There is one other question that some might think to be a difficulty for O, for it might seem that O raises a certain sort of paradox about justification. For O does not seem to prevent B, an omniscient being, from having a justification for all sorts of propositions which he does not believe – it just claims that any belief which B has is one which B justifiably holds. But then consider a case of this sort: B has a justification for p_3, even though B does not believe that p_3. None the less, B does justifiably believe that he has a justification for p_3, and hence uses p_3 as part of his justification for p_4. But, since p_3 is not one of B's beliefs, it follows that p_3 is false. But if one's justification for a certain proposition includes a false proposition, doesn't it follow that the justification is defective? And further, suppose that p_4 is true, and thus that B believes p_4 and justifiably believes it. Wouldn't a case of this sort be a case in which B has a justified true belief, but does not have knowledge?

I think not. For, if p_3 is not believed by B, it is false; and, if it is false, there is another proposition which is true – namely, that p_3 is false. B then believes that p_3 is false, and further justifiably believes that p_3 is false. But, the assumption of the above purported difficulty for O is that p_3 itself had a justification for B at t. Now, a very plausible condition of adequacy on a theory of justification is this: a theory of justification J is adequate only if J does not allow, for any propositions p and *not-p*, that both p and *not-p* are justified for any person S at time t. The conjunction of these two claims (that both *not-p$_3$* and p_3 itself are justified for B) violates the condition of adequacy just given; and thus the above paragraph poses no real difficulty for O.

So, the standard conception of omniscience is not faulty on the grounds discussed above. It provides a plausible interpretation of what it is for a being to be all-knowing or omniscient, and it does so without requiring that such knowledge be different in kind from our more limited knowledge. In one sense, it is different, for we do not need to clarify a further condition for knowledge in order to avoid problems for a justified true belief account of knowledge. However, that nicety (a nicety because of the immense difficulty of clarifying such a condition) results from the fact that the concepts of justifiably believing all truths includes whatever fourth condition is necessary for knowledge for ordinary knowers. For, to justifiably believe a proposition requires that one has positive grounds or evidence for that belief and that one fails to have any non-overridden grounds for doubt concerning that belief. For any maximal and justified believer, any conditions which would undermine the satisfaction of a fourth condition for knowledge for ordinary believers would undermine the justification for such a maximal and justified believer, for those same conditions would be non-overridden grounds for doubt for a maximal believer. For example, in the Smith–Jones case, the underminer of knowledge is, plausibly, the claim that Jones does not own a Ford and has deceived Smith. However, any believer who believes all truths would already believe this proposition, not its negation as Smith does. Hence, if this claim undermines knowledge for such a maximal believer, it would have to be because he forms beliefs contrary to this information; but if any believer forms beliefs contrary to what he is aware of, those awarenesses are grounds for doubting the beliefs which he forms. Hence, the reason that we do not need to clarify a fourth condition in describing the knowledge of an omniscient being is that any such condition is included in the justification condition which has already been specified – in particular, in the clause of the justification condition which requires that there be no non-overridden grounds for doubting the belief in question. I conclude this section then with the claim that O does not suffer any deficiency because of its implications concerning the nature of knowledge. I turn now to O's purported difficulties concerning the objects of knowledge.

DIFFICULTIES FOR THE TRADITIONAL ACCOUNT

It will be recalled that the standard account of the objects of knowledge, that what is known is always and only a proposition, is a reductionistic account of the apparent diversity among the objects of intentional attitudes; for it would seem that the objects of our attitudes not only include propositions, but objects, persons, states of affairs, events, actions, and even possibilities. The alignment of the traditional account of omniscience with this reductionist view leads to the worry that the traditional account of omniscience will be untenable, given the worries that plague reductionist accounts in general: namely, that some of the apparent diversity resists standardisation in whatever favoured way prescribed by the reductionists. The first anti-reductionist worry in our context arises from *de re/de dicto* considerations.

The Problem of *De Re* Belief

Quine called our attention to the difference between believing that the tallest spy is a spy, and the more substantive relation between a believer and the tallest spy: believing of the tallest spy that he is a spy.[6] The first is a belief in a rather trivial truth, the second is clearly not.

We can make sense of this case with reference to the *de re/de dicto* distinction discussed earlier. There the distinction concerned whether necessity was predicated of a proposition or of an object; here the distinction seems to be a distinction between the object of belief being a proposition (believing that the tallest spy is a spy) or an individual (believing of the person who is the tallest spy, that he is a spy).

This distinction is a close cousin at least of Russell's earlier distinction between knowledge by acquaintance and knowledge by description.[7] Russell claims that all knowledge must be grounded in knowledge of things with which we are acquainted. All other knowledge is descriptive. One way to put this last point might be that knowledge that is not the result of acquaintance is knowledge of the relationship between various properties, for according to Russell descriptions are just predicates of a certain sort. Since if a predicate expresses anything it expresses or signifies a property, knowledge by description can be thought of as knowledge of the relations between properties. The final step here is to tie together knowledge of the relations between properties with propositions, and there are conceptions of propositions in which this is true. To say that Jack is mad implies a certain relation between the properties of being identical to Jack and being mad. (Russell, of course, would identify the ordinary proper name 'Jack' with a different description than 'being Jack', but that need not concern us here.)

Knowledge by acquaintance, though, cannot be reduced to relations between properties; for what one is acquainted with, according to Russell, is a particular. Particulars are not properties; they are the things which properties are properties of. Further, particulars are picked out by what Russell calls 'logically proper names'. Concerning awareness of such entities, Russell claims:

> Now although it is very difficult to define 'awareness', it is not at all difficult to say that I am aware of this, and that, and the other, and so on through a heterogeneous collection of objects. If I describe these objects, I may of course describe them wrongly; hence I cannot with certainty communicate to another what are the things of which I am aware. But if I speak to myself, and denote them by what may be called 'proper names', rather than by descriptive words, I cannot be in error ... There is thus at any given moment a certain assemblage of objects to which I could, if I chose, give proper names; these are the objects of my 'awareness', the objects 'before my mind', or the objects that are within my present 'experience'.[8]

If we were to take Russell's acquaintance/description distinction to be the distinction between *de re* and *de dicto* attitudes, we would say that a *de re* belief is one in which the object of that belief could be picked out by a logically proper name, i.e. by a name that lacked any descriptive content whatsoever. All other beliefs would count as *de dicto* beliefs. However, there are good reasons to keep Russell's distinction separate from the distinctions we are considering. On Russell's distinction, nothing can be an object of acquaintance unless it is completely unconceptualised. Such a view is plagued with serious difficulties surrounding the possibility of totally unconceptualised unawareness. Fortunately, the *de re/de dicto* distinction is not committed to the possibility of totally unconceptualised awareness – or at least, we should not start from the assumption that it is committed to such. There is no good reason to think, from the start, that *de re* attitudes need be completely unconceptualised.

Apparently, the reason for insisting that some particulars be picked out by logically proper names is so that an infallible ground of knowledge can be defended. As is obvious in the above quote, Russell's worry is that if the awareness implies any descriptive content, one may be mistaken about that content. Thus, there is another good reason to distinguish between Russell's distinction and the one we are considering, for our distinction is not motivated by epistemological concerns about certainty. What connection there is between our distinction and the epistemic notion of certainty is left open, to be considered after getting clear on the distinction itself. Russell's distinction is infected from the start with epistemological worries about certainty.

So there are reasons for leaving Russell's distinction behind, and in particular, there are good reasons for not assuming that the *de re/de dicto* distinction is a distinction between the completely unconceptualised and anything conceptualised even to a slight extent. A better strategy is to consider some clear examples of the distinction, and then attempt to evaluate the impact of these examples on the claim that *de re* attitudes are different in type and irreducible to *de dicto* attitudes.

The example which generated the original discussion of the distinction was Quine's distinction between believing that the tallest spy is a spy and believing of the tallest spy that he is a spy. One might think, on the basis of this example, that the distinction was a rather simple scope distinction. If we let '*Bs*' be a belief operator, and '*Ex*' the existential quantifier, we could say that the *de dicto* belief in question is symbolised as '$(Bs)(Ex)(x$ is $F\&G)$'; and the *de re* belief as '$(Ex)[(x = A)\&(Bs)(A$ is $G)]$'. So, the distinction in the tallest spy case is just the distinction between believing that there is a tallest spy who is a spy, and there really being a tallest spy (who is A) and one's believing that he, the one who as a matter of fact is the tallest spy, is a spy.

If this is all there is to the distinction, our account of omniscience is in no serious difficulty, for reducing *de re* beliefs to *de dicto* presents no problem given that the only difference between the two is the scope of the quantifiers. The reductive schema, much like Quine's original proposal, would then be:

R1:   *S* believes of *x* that it is *F* $=_{\text{df.}}$ (i) $x = A$, and (ii) *S* believes *A is F*.

Many, however, thought that this understanding was too permissive in that it made *de re* beliefs much too easy to have. For example, if there is a tallest spy and I believe that the tallest spy is a spy, then whether I am aware who he is or not, on R1 I believe of him that he is a spy. Yet, the lack of any sort of epistemic intimacy with the tallest spy would seem to suggest that I do not believe of him that he is a spy. The mere fact that an individuating description happens to pick out an individual should not imply that any trivial belief I have about what is implied by that description is really about the individual himself. Thus, R1 is too permissive.

Awareness of this difficulty with R1 led to attempts to restrict just when a denoting phrase could imply *de re* belief of the object denoted. So, for example, Kaplan suggests:

R2: *S* believes of *x* that it is *F* = df. (i) *S* believes that *A* is *F*, (ii) 'b' is the word in *S*'s language that refers to *A*, and 'b' represents *x* for *S*.[9]

What is it for a word to represent an object for a person? Kaplan claims that the word must be a 'vivid' name for that object for the person; it must be part of the internal story he tells to himself when thinking about that object.

Sosa's proposal is somewhat different, but is still an attempt to restrict under what conditions a denoting term signals a *de re* belief. He claims:

R3: *S* believes of *x* that it is $F =_{\text{df.}}$ *S* believes that *A* is *F*, 'b' is the word in *S*'s language that refers to *A*, and 'b' is a distinguished term for *S*.[10]

What is it for a term to be a distinguished term for *S*? According to Sosa, it is not easy to say, for there are pragmatic elements to the notion of a term's being distinguished. We can get an idea of what he has in mind, though, by considering his discussion of a particular case. If a spy sees an investigator checking out his locker, Sosa claims the spy is correct in thinking that the investigator is coming to hold beliefs about him. Why? Because the investigator comes to hold a belief under a singular term 'the owner of this locker', 'which would enable the investigator to track the spy down without much difficulty'.[11] A term is a distinguished term, then, when it is not only a name for an individual, but also when it enables a person to pick out easily, or track down, the individual in question.

It should be noted that R2 and R3 have different implications for the original tallest spy case. Whereas Sosa claims that R3 allows that, in ordinary cases, those who believe that the tallest spy is a spy also believe of the tallest spy that he is a spy, R2 does not allow this claim. R2 denies this claim because 'the tallest spy' is not a name for most people for the tallest spy. Yet it is a term which is distinguished; it does enable a person to "track down" fairly easily the person who is the tallest spy. Hence, R2 denies, and R3 allows, that those who believe that the tallest spy is a spy regularly believe of the tallest spy that he is a spy.

Noting the divergence between restrictive and permissible reductive accounts, Chisholm proposes that our ordinary locutions ascribing *de re* beliefs are systematically ambiguous between the more restrictive and less restrictive views.[12] He thus proposes two different reductive accounts, the first being roughly equivalent to R1. Noting that this understanding seems to allow too many *de re* beliefs, Chisholm grants that there is another sense of *de re* belief, a more restrictive sense, but one which can also be reduced to *de dicto* belief. His version of reductionism is:

R4: *S* believes of *x* that it is $F =_{df.}$ there is an individual concept *C* such that (i) *S* knows a proposition implying *x* to have *C* and (ii) *S* accepts a proposition which implies *x* to have *C* and *F*.[13]

In order to understand R4, we need several definitions. They are:

D1: *C* is an individual concept $=_{df.}$ *C* is a property such that (i) possibly, something has *C*, and (ii) it is not possible that more than one thing has *C* at a time.[14]

D2: *p* implies *x* to have $F =_{df.}$ there is a *G* such that (i) *G* is an individual concept, (ii) *p* entails the conjunction of *F* and *G*, and (iii) *x* has *G*.[15]

D3: *p* entails the property $F =_{df.}$ *p* is necessarily such that (i) if it obtains then something is *F*, and (ii) whoever accepts *p* believes that something is *F*.[16]

An individual concept, then, is just an individuator; it can apply to at most one thing at a time. Thus definite descriptions, such as 'the tallest spy', will be individual concepts. Since Chisholm introduces R4 to restrict ascriptions of *de re* beliefs, in particular to avoid allowing that everyone who thinks the tallest spy is a spy has a belief about the tallest spy himself, let us see what R4 implies regarding that example. Chisholm claims that not all who believe that the tallest spy is a spy, believe of the tallest spy that he is a spy, on R4. Why? Because, according to Chisholm, by (i) of R4, one must know that there is a tallest spy in order to have such a *de re* belief about him; and, according to Chisholm, that requires having information which it is doubtful that anyone has (one would have to know, for example, that there are not two spies who are equally tall). So, Chisholm says, R4 is sufficiently restrictive to handle the sorts of cases that are problematic on R1.

Burge's view is quite close to Chisholm's more restrictive conception. According to Burge, any belief is *de re* unless it is "completely conceptualized".[17] He does not bother to clarify what this phrase means, but I think we can understand it as follows. In order to avoid requiring that an object is the real object of one's belief, one must conceive that object under an individuating concept. In other words, one must be thinking of the object in a way that individuates that thing from all other things, and, further, this individuation must result from taking the object to fall under some property. Thus, it is only in connection with some property of the object that one ascribes to it some other property. Burge holds that then and only then do we fail to have *de re* beliefs.

Others, though, have even more restrictive conceptions of *de re* belief. Brand, for example, doubts that any of us have *de re* beliefs about Plato; he even wonders if we have *de re* beliefs about Nixon given that we have only seen him on television and never in person.[18] If Brand's worries are correct, if we really do not have *de re* beliefs in these cases, R4 as well as R2 and R3 are inadequate reductive attempts; for all three definitions allow that many of us have *de re* beliefs about these objects.

It is time to attempt to make some sense of these various conceptions of the distinction between *de re* and *de dicto* attitudes. There are, it seems to me, two quite different conceptions of what a *de re* attitude is like. First, there is the Quine–Kaplan–Burge camp that thinks of the distinction solely in logical, semantic, or linguistic terms. The problem is one within the philosophy of language for these individuals, and the plausibility or implausibility of reductionism of *de re* to *de dicto* is to be considered within strictures of a semantic, logical, or linguistic-conceptual sort. Quine construes the problem as a mere problem of scope, Kaplan attempts to accomplish the reduction by introducing a "vivid name" for the object, and Burge requires that *de re* belief is present unless a "complete conceptualisation" of the object in question is achieved.

In the other camp are Sosa, Chisholm, and Brand, and members of this camp conceive the distinction as involving epistemological elements. Brand's claim that none of us has *de re* beliefs about Plato and his worry that beliefs acquired through television do not result in *de re* beliefs are illustrative of the claims of this camp. We have no *de re* beliefs about Plato, and may not about Nixon, because we lack the right sort of *epistemic intimacy* with those individuals. Members of the epistemic intimacy camp do not simply claim that the logical–semantic–conceptual camp is wrong; rather, they claim that logical, conceptual, or semantic reductions will be insufficient in the absence of a requirement of epistemic intimacy with the object in question. Sosa requires that the semantic component of the reduction be one which will enable the person to "easily track down" the object in question, Chisholm requires that the person knows something that implies the object in question falls under the relevant individuating concept, and

Brand seems to want direct perceptual acquaintance with the object in question. In any case, members of this camp add some sort of epistemic intimacy requirements to the semantic, conceptual, or logical reductive requirements (hereafter I shall refer to the latter as the SCL requirement, and to the former as the EI requirement).

What are the implications here for principle O, the understanding of omniscience on which only knowledge of propositions is required? Given the above camps, four possibilities concerning *de re* belief appear: (i) neither the SCL nor the EI reductive requirements can be satisfied by (some class of) *de dicto* beliefs; (ii) the SCL requirement can be satisfied, but the EI requirement cannot be satisfied, by *de dicto* beliefs; (iii) the EI requirement can be satisfied, but the SCL requirement cannot be satisfied, by *de dicto* beliefs; or (iv) both the SCL and EI requirements can be satisfied by (some class of) *de dicto* beliefs.

Option (iv) has obvious implications for the standard conception of omniscience, for if (iv) is correct, the standard account is in no danger on the basis of the distinction between *de re* and *de dicto* beliefs. Also, if option (ii) is correct, O does not face serious difficulty. For even if there is no particular set of *de dicto* beliefs which can guarantee that a person has the right sort of epistemic intimacy with the object in question, O requires that the *de dicto* beliefs of any omniscient being do not lack epistemic components. As O states it, omniscience does not only require believing all truths, but *justifiably* believing them. Hence, even if one can fail to have some *de re* belief even though one believes all truths (in virtue of lacking the right sort of epistemic intimacy to the object in question), this point does not undermine O. For O not only requires that an omniscient being believes all truths, but that such a being justifiably believes all truths. Hence, if option (ii) correctly characterises the relationship between *de dicto* and *de re* belief, O already guarantees that any *de re* belief not identical to some set of *de dicto* beliefs is had by any omniscient being (in virtue of O's requirement of the epistemic intimacy necessary for justifiably believing all truths).

The only worry there could be here is if some special sort of epistemic intimacy were required, such as direct perceptual awareness (consider, for example, Brand's worries that seeing a person on television is not the right sort of epistemic intimacy). But why should one insist on such directness? Presumably, because the more indirect the channel, the greater the risk of loss or distortion of information. But, if this is the reason, there will be no worries regarding principle O, for any being omniscient by O has whatever sort of epistemic intimacy required that prevents any loss or distortion of information. Thus, even if some special sort of epistemic intimacy were required as the ground for the truth of option (ii), there is no reason to doubt the adequacy of O.

So, the real test for the standard conception of omniscience is whether the SCL requirement can be satisfied, for both the remaining options ((i) and (iii)) claim that it cannot. The strongest challenge to the claim that it can is Burge's insistence that, for it to be satisfied, the belief in question must be "fully conceptualized", and he claims that many beliefs cannot be construed as fully conceptualized. Hence, reductionism from *de re* to *de dicto* attitudes is not possible.

Let us consider a rather simple example in order to evaluate the plausibility of Burge's claim on behalf of non-reductionism – say, a four-year-old saying, 'That ball is yellow', and believing what he says about a ball directly in front of him on the floor. As I have explicated the notion of full conceptualisation, Burge wishes to insist that, in order for this *de re* belief to be reducible to *de dicto*, there must be some individuating concept under which the child conceives the ball. Some perhaps plausible candidates might be: the thing I am pointing to, the thing I am calling attention to, the thing right in front of me, etc. Yet, Burge might claim, none of these concepts need be part of the conscious thoughts of the child; in fact, he may believe that the ball is yellow and not even have the concept of pointing (though, of course, he can point), or of calling attention to something (though, again, he can call attention to things), or of being in front of one. Hence, the belief is not fully conceptualised, for the object is not distinguished for the child from all other things by some concept under which he is thinking of the object.

Suppose we grant that Burge is correct here, both about the lack of complete conceptualisation and the requirement that complete conceptualisation is necessary for *de dicto* belief. Does it follow that the standard conception of omniscience must be abandoned? To see that the child's belief causes no problems, we need only consider the difference between the child's belief and the belief his parent has about the ball when she believes that the ball in question is yellow. Suppose that she does individuate the ball in question as the ball that is right in front of her, the one to which she is directing her attention. It follows then that she and her child do not have identical beliefs: after all, hers is a belief about a fully conceptualised object and her child's belief is not. Yet, it would be wrong to infer from this fact that the content of the child's belief is completely distinct from the content of the mother's. Even if the two beliefs are not identical, there is nothing in the content of the child's belief that is not included in the content of the mother's belief. The lesson here is that even if *de re* beliefs can occur, there is no special content to such beliefs that are not included in beliefs which are fully conceptualised beliefs about the same object. My point is that if a belief is a fully conceptualised one and the person in question bears the same relation of epistemic intimacy to the object in question, that person's belief will include any content which is included in a less than fully conceptualised belief of a person in that epistemically intimate context.

So, even if the SCL requirement cannot be met in such a way as to allow that *de re* belief is reducible to *de dicto*, this fact does not undermine O. For the way in which such a reduction would fail shows only that a *de re* belief can fail to include any appropriate *de dicto* belief. Principle O, though, does not require the reducibility thesis; it only requires that, if there are *de re* beliefs that are not reducible, the irreducible elements can be included in the beliefs of complete conceptualisers in appropriate epistemically intimate relations to the object in question. And this claim is quite plausible, as we have seen in the mother–child case above.

Hence, the distinction between *de re* and *de dicto* beliefs does not present a problem for O, the traditional account of omniscience. If *de re* beliefs are only partially reducible to *de dicto* (this is option (ii) above), a person can still know all there is to know by knowing all true propositions. Further, even if *de re* beliefs are completely irreducible to *de dicto* beliefs (option (i) above), it does not follow that a complete conceptualiser lacks anything which a *de re* believer has except epistemic intimacy to the object in question. The point is that even if we can correctly attribute beliefs to individuals lacking the individuating concepts in question, we should not think that such individuals are aware of a content unavailable to more robust conceptualisers. Of course, the content of the beliefs of complete conceptualisers is not identical to the content of the beliefs of less adequate conceptualisers, but the point is not one of identity but rather one of inclusion; and we have seen no reason to think that the content of a complete conceptualiser's belief does not include the content of a less adequate conceptualiser's belief. Hence, I conclude that whether *de re* attitudes are only partially reducible, or completely irreducible, to *de dicto* attitudes, the traditional conception of omniscience captured in principle O remains unscathed.

Yet the *de re/de dicto* distinction may not pose the most serious challenge to the standard account. Recently, philosophers have become sensitive to the difference between believing of something (even if that thing is oneself) that it has a certain property and believing of oneself, in the context of being aware that the object of belief is oneself, that oneself has a certain property. This is the problem of *de se* belief, and it is to this problem that we now turn.

The Problem of *De Se* Belief

Consider Perry's account of how the problem of *de se* belief arises:

> I once followed a trail of sugar on a supermarket floor, pushing my cart down the aisle on one side of a tall counter and back the aisle on the other, seeking the shopper with the torn sack to tell him he was making a mess. But I seemed unable to catch up. Finally it dawned on me. I was the shopper I was trying to catch.
>
> I believed at the outset that the shopper with a torn sack was making a mess. And I was right. But I didn't believe that I was making a mess. That seems to be something I came to believe. And when I came to believe that, I stopped following the trail around the counter, and rearranged the torn sack in my cart. My change in beliefs seems to explain my change in behavior.[19]

Perry, in the course of his meanderings, makes a discovery; the discovery that the shopper with the torn sack is he himself. A possible description of this discovery is that, whereas he originally believed *de dicto* that the shopper with the torn sack is making a mess, he comes to have a *de re* belief with himself as the object in question, so that he comes to believe of himself that he is making a mess.

But things are not that simple. Perry wishes to argue that the change in his beliefs cannot be accounted for simply on the basis of the *de re/de dicto* distinction. He claims that the change in his beliefs has essential reference to indexicals. He claims:

> Suppose I had said, in the manner of de Gaulle, 'I came to believe that John Perry is making a mess.' I would no longer have explained why I stopped and looked in my own cart. To explain that I would have to add, 'and I believe that I am John Perry,' bringing in the indexical again. After all, suppose I had really given my explanation in the manner of de Gaulle, and said 'I came to believe that de Gaulle is making a mess.' That wouldn't have explained my stopping at all. But it really would have explained it every bit as much as 'I came to believe John Perry is making a mess'. For if I added 'and I believe that I am de Gaulle' the explanations would be on par. The only

reason 'I came to believe John Perry is making a mess' seems to explain my action is our natural assumption that I did believe I was John Perry and didn't believe I was de Gaulle. So replacing the indexical 'I' with another term designating the same person really does, as claimed, destroy the explanation.[20]

The point of this discussion is not hard to see. Surely picking out oneself by a proper name is sufficient for *de re* belief on any reasonable conception of such beliefs; yet we cannot explain Perry's behaviour merely by noting that he moved from having a *de dicto* belief about the shopper with a torn bag to a *de re* belief about John Perry. In addition, what is necessary is his awareness that he himself is John Perry, i.e. he must come to believe (*de se*) that he is John Perry. There seemingly is something in addition to *de re* and *de dicto* belief; there are also the beliefs that we have about ourselves which seem to be quite different from the other two.

It must be granted that it is one thing to have a belief about an object and quite another thing to have a belief about oneself. It is one thing to note of the person whose reflection one sees in the mirror that his pants are on fire; it is quite another thing to note that that person is onself, and thereby to note that one's own pants are on fire. Yet the claim to be considered here is not whether the beliefs are different, but rather whether the difference raises problems for a propositional construal of omniscience. So, we must ask, does the issue of *de se* belief raise problems for our account of omniscience?

The initial appearance is that no such problems are created, for it appears that *de se* belief is straightforwardly reducible to *de dicto*. For example, if I believe that I am making a mess, I am believing something that implies that there is a property, *being identical with me*, which is mutually instantiated with the property *being such that one is making a mess*. What property is the property of being identical with me? Presumably, it is my essence or haecceity.[21] So, what I am believing is merely a *de dicto* claim which implies that special property, my essence, is mutually instantiated with some other property.

De Se *Belief and Private Propositions*

So the propositionalist can carry through the reduction of *de se* to *de dicto*, but it would appear that the reduction does not come without a price. To see the apparent cost, consider Chisholm's carefully developed defence of the propositional view. He first explains how individuation of self occurs:

If I do individuate myself *per se* then there are propositions which are such that: I know them to be true; they imply some property that I have uniquely; and they do not imply any property that any *other* individual thing has uniquely. What property, then, could it be that I thus know myself to have uniquely and that does not pick me out merely by relating me uniquely to some other individual thing? It can only be the property of *being me*, or *being identical with myself*.[22]

Chisholm then explains what this property is:

The property of *being me*, of *being identical with myself*, can only be an individual essence or haeccity. It is a property I cannot fail to have. And it is a property that is 'repugnant to' all other things – 'repugnant' in the sense that nothing diverse from me could possibly have it.[23]

Finally, Chisholm explains the sort of theory which he thinks is implied by the above discussion:

The theory of the use of the first person pronoun – for example, 'I' – that fits most naturally with what I have suggested is the following. Each person who uses the first person pronoun uses it to refer to himself and in such a way that, in that use, its *Bedeutung* or reference is himself and its *Sinn* or intention is his own individual essence. A corollary would be that, whereas each person knows directly and immediately certain propositions implying his own individual essence, no one knows any propositions implying the individual essence of anyone else.[24]

Chisholm here describes precisely the view that I have suggested the propositionalist must take. He must claim that the property expressed by the use of the first person pronoun is just the property of being identical with the person using that pronoun. The bothersome dimension of the view is Chisholm's claim that the view has a corollary – that no one knows any propositions implying the individual essence of anyone else. Though the passages quoted do not explicitly state it, this corollary is more accurately put as the claim that no one knows, believes, entertains, or takes any intentional attitude to any propositions implying the individual essence of anyone else; hence, if Chisholm is right, some propositions are private propositions, in the sense that only some persons can have access to those propositions.

This corollary may not be bothersome to some people, but in the context of this investigation, it is extremely problematic. For, on the traditional account, a being is omniscient if and only if that being knows all true propositions. Yet if there are private propositions, then it is impossible that any being be omniscient if the traditional account of omniscience is correct.

I do not mean to suggest that it is impossible to alter the traditional account in such a way that it is still plausible to hold that there is an omniscient being (even though there are some propositions – namely, private ones – which that being does not know). Yet, the alterations necessary are not simple. We cannot, for example, alter the claim so that a being is omniscient if and only if that being knows all propositions it is capable of knowing. Rocks know nothing and cannot know anything; on this alteration, they would be omniscient. Nor can we suggest that a being is omniscient if it knows as many true propositions as can be known. Since there are infinitely many true propositions, a being could be omniscient by this definition even though there were infinitely many true and accessible propositions which it did not know. This follows since all denumerably infinite sets are of the same size. Finally, we cannot accept a limited doctrine of omniscience on which a being is omniscient if and only if that being knows everything that can be known. First, the private propositions in question can be known. Worse, the objections from Chapter 1 against such a limited doctrine show that even if it could handle the problem of private propositions, it would be inadequate on other grounds. So it is not easy to see how to alter the doctrine of omniscience so that a being can be omniscient even though there are private propositions.

That there are no simple ways to reconstrue the doctrine does not give a very strong reason for being dissatisfied with a theory which implies the existence of private propositions. But the above reason is not the only reason for being dissatisfied with private propositions. Another is that Christians and other theists should think of God as being most aware of our natures. In fact, He surely knows us better than we know ourselves. Yet, if we accept the doctrine of private propositions, it would seem that we are committed to denying this point. If only we can grasp our essences, then there is an intimacy we have with our natures that God does not. Hence, I suggest, theists ought to be interested in denying the privacy of any proposition.

There are also philosophical reasons for rejecting a theory which includes private propositions. First, if we can get along without positing them, we should, i.e. if we can develop a theory as adequate as a theory which posits private propositions, we should accept the theory that fails to imply the existence of private propositions. Another reason for rejecting private propositions is that it is intuitively obvious that there are no such propositions. When my wife says 'I have a dentist appointment today,' I might correctly say, 'I know that.' What do I know? I know that what she asserted is true; yet if there are private propositions, she asserted one, and hence I could not know that what she asserted is true. Yet, since we can know what a person asserts about himself or herself, there can be no private propositions.

There have been several other attempts besides Chisholm's to solve the riddle of first-person indexicals without giving up the propositional view, and it is noteworthy that each of them provides little comfort to the defender of the traditional view of omniscience. Anscombe, for example, claims first-person indexical sentences express propositions with demonstrative elements. So, for example, she claims that 'I am this thing here' means 'this thing here is the person of whose action this idea of action is an idea, of whose movements these ideas of movement are ideas, of whose posture this is the idea'.[25] Yet, this view offers little hope for the defender of the traditional view of omniscience. As Chisholm notes, 'It is clear that she cannot explicate my use of 'I' in this way, and I think she might concede that she cannot grasp my 'I' propositions at all.'[26] The account of the meaning of 'I am this thing here' works only if the reference of the word 'I' is the author of that sentence, for if it is not, it is not clear how reference for the occurrences of 'this' in the translational equivalent is to be secured. What she would say about the meaning of that sentence in the third-person case, i.e. when, for example, she is trying to explain what I mean when I use that sentence, is not clear. Perhaps Chisholm is right that she would admit that there are private propositions; in any case, we lack a comprehensive enough account of 'I' for the defender of the traditional account of omniscience to be comfortable in thinking that private propositions have been avoided by Anscombe's views.

Castaneda's view straightforwardly implies the existence of private propositions. He claims that when a person uses an 'I'-sentence, he expresses an 'I'-proposition which 'is different from every third-person proposition about him, and, of course, different from any third-person proposition about anything else'.[27] Castaneda goes on to claim that these first-person propositions are contingent: they exist if and only if the person in question exists.[28] That complication, though, is irrelevant to our concerns; for whether the propositions are contingent or not does not affect the point that, since first-person propositions are unique in the way Castaneda describes them, no one but the person whom a particular proposition is about could grasp them. This follows since, for Castaneda, no first-person proposition is identical to any third-person proposition. Thus, on Castaneda's view as well, we are stuck with private propositions.

A Way Out?

Though the propositional theory seems committed to private propositions, perhaps some diagnostic work concerning the nature of propositions will aid us in finding a way out of this apparent implication. The propositional theory we have been assuming seems committed to several claims. First, on the standard view, it is claimed that:

(6) The content of any intentional attitude is a propositional content.

Further, though no explicit definition of a proposition is offered, several principles govern the notion:

(7) If p is a proposition, then p is either true or false, but not both.
(8) If p is a proposition, p is composed of properties, where this notion of compositional is to be understood as:

> D5: p is composed of properties $r_1 \ldots r_n$, where n is less than or equal to $1 =_{df.} p$ is a proposition implying the mutual instantiation of $r_1 \ldots r_n$.

(9) If p is a proposition, then p exists in every possible world.

As we saw above, Castaneda denies (9), but his view is no more helpful because of that denial than it would have been otherwise. There is, however, another recent attempt to provide an alternative propositional view to Chisholm's, one which on the face of it at least does not require private propositions. This attempt, in effect, abandons both (9) and (7). Sosa claims that one way to avoid some difficulties with the propositional view is to think of (some) propositions as variant in truth-value. He claims:

> A further alternative is offered by a *theory of perspectives* ... According to the theory of perspectives only some propositions are true or false independently of any perspective (objectively, absolutely). In addition to such unperspectival propositions, however, there are also perspectival propositions, and these may be true in one perspective or from one standpoint and false in another perspective

or from another standpoint. Thus the proposition expressed by the English sentence 'I am now sitting' may be true in the perspective defined by you at noon today, whereas it is false in the perspective defined by me at midnight tonight.

A perspective is an ordered pair whose first member is a thing and whose second member is a time. Perspectival propositions are those that would be expressed either by sentences in the first person singular or with tensed verbs.[29]

Sosa's view seems to avoid the privacy problem, for when you believe what is expressed by the sentence 'I'm tired', you are believing exactly what I believe when I believe what is expressed by that sentence. Thus, if we agree to call what is expressed here a 'first-person proposition', we are believing the same first person proposition; hence, that proposition cannot be a private proposition.

Intuitively, this view is problematic. When I believe what is expressed by the sentence 'I'm tired', I am not believing the same thing as you believe when you believe what is expressed for you by the sentence 'I'm tired'. I believe something about *me*; you do not believe something about me, rather you believe something about *you*.

There are other problems with the view as well. One dilemma which the perspectival view faces concerns the notion of truth which it posits. The perspectival view claims that (some) propositions are not true or false, but are only true or false at a perspective. Perhaps it would be best to hyphenate the notions – true-at-(S,t); false-at-(S,t) – in order to make clear that these notions are technical notions in need of clarification. One way to clarify these notions is analogous to the way we take a sentence, such as 'it is raining', to express a proposition which is true or false *simpliciter*: we say that what is really expressed is the proposition that it is raining at a particular place and time. So, one might clarify the technical notion in question in terms of the ordinary notion of truth.

Yet, if such an explication is given, the perspectival view would no longer be able to avoid the problem of private propositions. Take any perspectival proposition p, and suppose it is agreed that when that proposition is true-at-a-perspective, there is some other non-perspectival proposition q which is true *simpliciter*. Further, suppose that p is about Jim. Now, since q clarifies what it is for p to be true at a perspective, we can assume that Jim believes p if and only if he believes q. But, unless q is a private proposition, believing it will not explain the difference between mere *de re* awareness of self and *de se* awareness of self; for if q is not a private proposition, there is no reason to think that

Jim cannot believe it without being aware of himself as himself. Thus, it would seem, the notion of truth-at-a-perspective can be clarified in terms of truth *simpliciter* only at the expense of reintroducing private propositions.

Sosa suggests that there is some connection between his technical notion and the ordinary notion of truth. He says:

> Note that if a proposition is believed, it is always believed in the perspective defined by the believer and the time of belief. This enables us to define the truth of a belief as the proposition believed in *the perspective in which it is believed*.
>
> Thus if I believe now that I am wise, my belief is true if (a) I believe a certain proposition (which is the one that anyone must believe at any given time in order to believe of himself as himself and of that time as the time then present that he is then wise), and (b) that proposition is true in the perspective in which I then believe it, the perspective defined by myself (the believer) and the present time (the time of belief).[30]

It might appear that this passage contains a clarification of the technical notion of truth-at-a-perspective, yet it does not. At best, it shows how to define another technical notion (the truth of a belief) in terms of truth-at-a-perspective. The notion of the truth of a belief is just as much a technical notion as the notion of truth-at-a-perspective, for it is, strictly speaking, semantic elements that are true or false. So, at best, it would be the semantic content of a belief that is true or false, since beliefs have semantic elements as their contents, but are not themselves semantic elements.

Notice that we cannot take this passage as a clarification of truth-at-a-perspective for another reason. Presumably, many properties are exemplified by me at present about which I do not have beliefs. Hence, they are true at the perspective defined by me, now. Yet I do not believe them, hence we cannot define truth-at-a-perspective in terms of the truth of what I believe.

Or again, if beliefs are the only things that can have the property of being true-at-a-perspective, Sosa will have a hard time explaining how what one hopes for, wishes for, etc., can be true. In some cases the explanation will be simple: when one hopes for peace in Israel, for example, it may be that what one hopes for is simply true (not true-at-a-perspective). Yet suppose I hope that I am wise and it happens that I am wise. Can we then say that what I hoped for is true? We cannot say this unless we can define the technical notion of a truth-at-a-perspective in terms other than the notion of the truth of a belief.

Thus it would seem that it is not clear at all that we can clarify truth-at-a-perspective in terms of the ordinary notion of truth without introducing many other problems. Given these problems, perhaps one might attempt to take the locution 'true-at-(S,t)' as undefined. There are problems here as well though. First, it is bad philosophical practice to introduce a technical notion and then take it as undefined. Much progress could be made if this approach were allowed – any time a problem arose, we could invent a technical term which, happily, is the solution. The problem is that without some clarification we have no idea what the solution comes to, and with Sosa's technical notion, any way I can see of clarifying it raises other equally severe problems.

Further, if we take truth-at-a-perspective as undefined and cannot define it in terms of ordinary truth, we undermine the entailment relation between *I am now wise* and *someone is wise*; for what it means for one proposition to entail another is that it is impossible for the first to be true and the second false. As far as I can see, there is no understanding of truth in terms of truth-at-a-perspective forthcoming except at the overly high price of private propositions. Hence Sosa's view faces a dilemma. If there is no connection between truth and truth-at-a-perspective, it is hard to see what it might mean to hold that *I am now wise* entails *someone is wise*, for entailment is defined in terms of the impossibility of one proposition being true while another is false. What seems to follow, instead, is that every perspectival proposition entails every other proposition, since, because it is impossible for any perspectival proposition to be true, it is thereby impossible for such a proposition to be true while any other is false. So we have another reason to reject the perspectival theory. The alternative to this conclusion is to find some way to clarify truth-at-a-perspective in terms of ordinary truth; but that, we have seen, lands us right back in the problem of private propositions.

In all, the problems for Sosa's perspectival theory seem insurmountable. We cannot clarify the technical notion it introduces, for in so doing, we raise many problems. Further, if we do not clarify the technical notion, other problems arise. For one, certain entailment relations no longer hold; and for another, it is not clear what sort of philosophical progress such a practice gives.

The perspectival theory, in spite of its problems, does have some intuitive attractiveness, though. For, doesn't it seem quite obvious that when each of two persons say 'I am tired', they have said the same thing even though we cannot describe what was said as being true or false *simpliciter*? All we can say, it might be claimed, is that what was said is true or false given the circumstances of utterance. And doesn't this last notion come to much the same thing as the perspectival theory?

This last paragraph gives what I take to be the strongest intuitive foundation for the perspectival theory, and it is important to notice that using the above consideration to support the perspectival theory rests on a confusion. It may be true that when two different persons express their beliefs with first-person indexical sentences, the meaning of their utterances is the same. But we should not confuse what proposition is expressed by a sentence with what that sentence means. Propositions are introduced for both Sosa and myself as the bearers of truth; it is an interesting, and I think false, philosophical thesis that the bearers of truth are the meanings of the sentences in question. Propositions are abstract entities, and they have the characteristic of being true or false; meanings are properties of words, sentences, phrases, and other linguistic (non-abstract) entities. Perhaps at bottom, this is the confusion underlying the perspectival theory: the confusion between a property of that which a sentence (with a particular meaning) expresses (the truth of a proposition) and a property of the sentence itself (the meaning of the sentence).

So far as I can see, then, the alternatives in the literature on the problem of the *he, himself* locution which defend a propositional account do not solve the problems raised by that locution. Perhaps, instead of trying to preserve the propositional view of self-awareness, we should try a different approach to solving the riddle of self-awareness. Recently, just such a strategy has been proposed by several philosophers who have considered this problem.[31] One of these is Chisholm, who has come to recant on his defence of the propositional view. Perhaps by considering his reasons for rejecting that view, we can clarify whether the traditional construal of omniscience is defective.

Chisholm's New View

Chisholm's response to the problem of the 'he, himself' locution is to suggest that we are attempting to explicate things in the wrong direction. Instead of attempting to explicate the 'he, himself' locution as a type of *de re* or *de dicto* proposition, Chisholm's suggestion is that we attempt to explicate these latter in terms of the former. He says:

Let us use the term 'emphatic reflexive' for the 'he, himself' locution

... and let us use 'non-emphatic reflexive' for those locutions ... that do not imply the 'he, himself', or emphatic, reflexive ... Now there are two ways of interpreting the significance of this distinction. In either case, we ask: 'Why is it that the non-emphatic reflexive (for example, Q) does not imply the corresponding emphatic reflexive (for example, S)?' But in the one case, we would trace the failure of implication to certain peculiarities of the emphatic reflexive. We would try to exhibit the emphatic reflexive as a special case of the non-emphatic reflexive. Whereas in the other case, we would proceed in the opposite direction: we would try to exhibit the non-emphatic reflexive as a special case of the emphatic reflexive. If we take the second approach, we will deny that the emphatic reflexive presents us with any unique logical structure. We will say that the failure of implication is due, rather to certain familiar facts about intentionality – as exhibited in the non-emphatic reflexive.

I suggest that, by exploring the possibility that the second approach is correct, we may arrive at a view enabling us to understand the logic of the two types of reflexive.[32]

So Chisholm claims that we can exhibit, in his words, the non-emphatic reflexive as a special instance of the emphatic reflexive. How does his theory work? Chisholm claims that when one has an intentional attitude, one's attitude is directed, not at a proposition, but at a property. Further, the *de se* form of each attitude is primary; the *de re* and *de dicto* forms are to be explicated in terms of the *de se* form.

Chisholm's theory includes the claim that the *de se* form is primary by taking the notion of direct attribution as undefined. This undefined notion is governed by two principles, according to Chisholm:

P1:   For every x, every y and every z, if x directly attributes z to y, then x is identical with y.

P2:   For every x, every y and ever z, if x directly attributes z to y, then z is a property.[33]

Given P1 and P2, we can define the *de se* form of belief as:

D6:   *S* believes that he himself is $F =_{df.}$ the property of being F is such that S directly attributes it to S.[34]

The *de dicto* form of belief is then defined as:

D7:   The state of affairs that p is accepted (*de dicto*) by $S =_{df.}$ there is one and only one state of affairs that p; and either (a) *S* directly attributes to S the property of being such that p, or (b) S indirectly attributes to the state of affairs that p, as the thing he is conceiving in a certain way, the property of being true.[35]

In order to understand D7, we need to understand indirect attribution:

D8: y is such that, as the thing that S bears R to, S indirectly attributes to it the property of being $F =_{df.} S$ bears R to y and only to y; and S directly attributes to S a property which entails the property of bearing R to just one thing and to a thing that is F.[36]

So to attribute indirectly the property of being true to a proposition is to stand in some indentifying relation to that proposition – perhaps that proposition is the proposition which one is presently thinking about, for example. Given that there is such an identifying relation, one indirectly attributes a property to it by directly attributing to oneself a property which entails both bearing the identifying relation to that proposition and the property of that proposition. Thus I might directly attribute to myself the property of being such that the proposition I am now considering (*I am working*) is true. This property entails that the proposition *I am working* bears an identifying relation to me and has the property of being true.

I shall not discuss Chisholm's explication of *de re* belief in terms of direct and indirect attribution; suffice it to say for now that he claims to have accomplished the task. It will be remembered from our earlier discussion that Chisholm thinks there are two senses of *de re* belief: one latidudinarian and the other more restrictive. Thus, we can expect two different construals of *de re* belief from Chisholm.

There are two central claims in Chisholm's new theory. The first, and perhaps most important in the context of the traditional account of omniscience, is that the propositional account of the contents of intentional attitudes is to be abandoned in favour of a property view. So, according to Chisholm, not only are we to explicate belief in terms of directly attributing properties to oneself, we are also to explicate wishing, wanting, considering, and other intention attitudes on this same model. The second point is that the direction of explanation is to be altered: instead of attempting to explain self-awareness in terms of the awareness of other sorts of things, self-awareness is taken to be the fundamental sort of awareness with all other awareness being defined in terms of it.

It is regarding this second claim that Chisholm's theory is most clearly defective. To see this, we need only note that there is a difference between an impossible state of affairs and a state of affairs which could never be truly believed to obtain.[37] For example, consider the difference between Descartes' considering his own non-existence and Descartes' considering the non-existence of God. If the usual understanding of God is allowed, the latter comes to Descartes' considering an impossible state of affairs; yet his considering his own non-existence is not a consideration of the same sort of affairs. If it were, then Descartes himself would be a necessary being, and he surely is not. The proper way to express what he is considering is a state of affairs which he could never truly believe to obtain.

The mistake made by Chisholm's reductionism is just the mistake involved in confusing the two sorts of states of affairs above. If indirect attribution is claimed to be reducible to direct attribution for all intentional attitudes, as Chisholm claims, one will be unable to distinguish between taking certain intentional attitudes towards impossible states of affairs and taking those same intentional attitudes towards possible states of affairs which are merely such that they could never be truly believed not to obtain. Imagine Descartes' considering his own non-existence. If the property view is correct, then what Descartes is considering is some property that he directly attributes to himself which includes his own non-existence. On this view, then, Descartes is considering himself to have a property which implies his own non-existence. Such a property is an impossible property: there is nothing that could exemplify it. Yet there is a state of affairs including the non-existence of Descartes which is possible. Hence the reductionistic attempt of the property view is bound to fail; it inevitably confuses some possible states of affairs with impossible ones. It requires saying that when one considers one's own non-existence, one is considering something that couldn't possibly be.

So we can see that taking self-awareness as primary and attempting to define other sorts of awarenesses in terms of it does not seem especially promising. However, this aspect of Chisholm's new theory is not as threatening to the traditional construal of omniscience as is its other aspect: namely, the abandoning of the propositional theory in favour of a property theory. Further, even if Chisholm's property theory is unsatisfactory on the grounds stated above, it does not follow that any property theory will be inadequate, for there is no good reason to think that any property theory must take self-awareness to be the primary sort of awareness (as Chisholm does).

We ought, then, to consider what sorts of reasons might be given for preferring a property view to a propositional view. Chisholm's view is that the propositional view ought to be abandoned on grounds of ontological economy.[38] The propositional view commits one to the existence of individual essences, the property theory does not; hence the property theory is superior to the propositional theory.

This reason is not especially strong. The property theory posits some special sort of ability persons have – the ability to directly attribute a property – which the propositional view does not. If entities are not to be posited beyond necessity, neither are abilities.

On the other hand, if the propositional view must posit private propositions as Chisholm and others have claimed, it is inadequate; and if the propositional view has this sort of inadequacy, there would be good reason to favour a property theory. Thus even though Chisholm's ontological economy argument does not give us sufficient reason to abandon the propositional view, we may have sufficient reason anyway because of the apparent tie between the propositional view and private propositions. So far, though, we have only seen that several philosophers either claim or imply that there is such a tie; before giving up on the propositional view, though, we ought to see whether any reasons other than purely testimonial ones can be marshalled to show that such a tie truly exists. I suggest that we take a closer look at the purported connection between the propositional view and the existence of private propositions.

Does a Propositional Theory Imply Private Propositions?

Chisholm's claim in a passage quoted earlier (on page 49) is that 'each person knows directly and immediately certain propositions implying his own individual essence'. His exact formulation of the corollary of this view is that 'no one knows any propositions implying the individual essence of anyone else', though it is clear that Chisholm intends to deny the possibility of having any sort of intentional attitude towards any propositions implying the individual essence of anything else. If we can agree that grasping a proposition is an essential component of having any intentional attitude towards a proposition, then, properly formulated, the corollary is:

COR1:   No one can grasp any proposition whose content implies the individual essence of any other thing.

Our question is what reasons can be given for thinking that COR1 is true, given that one accepts a propositional theory. One possible argument can be derived from the way Chisholm formulates the nature of self-awareness. His formulation is given in the first passage quoted earlier (on page 49) where he claims that individuation of self *per se* involves adopting an attitude towards propositions with three characteristics. First, such propositions are known to be true; second, they imply a property oneself has uniquely, i.e. one's essence; and third, they imply no property that anything else has uniquely. This formulation suggests that Chisholm is thinking that self-awareness is to be defined as:

SA1: S has self-awareness of $R =_{df.}$ (i) S knows that p; (ii) p implies the individual essense of R; and (iii) p implies no property other than the individual essence of R which anything other than R has uniquely.

Since it is a necessary truth that no one has self-awareness of anyone but themselves and since SA1 alone does not imply that S is identical to R, if SA1 is the proper account of self-awareness, then it must be combined with COR1 in order to account for the necessity of the claim that no one has self-awareness of anyone but themselves. Hence the following sort of argument appears for COR1. Since SA1 is correct, and since it alone does not imply that self awareness of something other than oneself is impossible, an additional principle is needed to show that such awareness is impossible. COR1 in conjunction with SA1 has the implication in question, and further no additional principle that fails to imply COR1 could have the required implication. Hence COR1 must be affirmed to give a proper account of self-awareness.

Whether this argument would be taken by Chisholm to be a proper representation of his reasons for thinking that COR1 is in fact a corollary of the propositional view, I am not sure. In any case, it might seem that the conclusion can be avoided merely by altering the account of self-awareness. For example, consider the following alternative account of self-awareness:

SA2: S has self-awareness of $R =_{df.}$ (i) S believes that p; (ii) p implies the individual essence of R; and (iii) the individual essence of S is identical to the individual essence of R.[39]

SA2 alone implies that no one can have self-awareness of anything but themselves; hence, if we accept SA2 rather than SA1, we have no need to affirm COR1. Further, SA2 does not imply that God cannot know propositions implying our essences; hence, if SA2 is adequate, we need not give up the traditional account of omniscience.

There is, though, a difficulty for this account of self-awareness.

Suppose we accept SA2 and grant that essences are not graspable only by the individual in question, i.e. each of us can grasp each other's essences, and in particular, God grasps them all. If this is so, SA2 fails to explain the earlier case of looking in the mirror and believing the proposition expressed by 'his pants are on fire'. Presumably if grasping the essence of another person is ever possible, such grasping occurs in this context; yet, unknown to the person in question, the person in the mirror is himself. Hence, by SA2, he has self-awareness even though he does not know that the person in the mirror is himself. This implication is incorrect; he comes to have self awareness only when he comes to recognise that he himself is the person in the mirror whose pants are on fire.

The only way to rescue SA2 from this counter-example and avoid the problem of private propositions is to hold that no one but God can grasp the individual essence of another thing. One might then claim that, in the pants-on-fire case, the person in question has the same relation to himself that persons normally have to another person – namely, a relation in which the individual essence in question is not grasped. None the less, God can grasp every individual essence, for if He cannot, then we are still left with the problem of private propositions.

This solution is not wholly satisfactory, for it runs afoul of the case cited earlier concerning my wife's assertion that she has a dentist appointment. If the above account is accurate, then what she asserted is, strictly speaking, something I could not have known. Yet it is obvious that I can know that what she asserted is true, hence the above account cannot be adequate.

Still, even if we cannot accept SA2, there is another way out of the above argument, a way hinted at in Chisholm's original statement of the corollary. His actual words are, 'A corollary would be that, whereas each person knows directly and immediately certain propositions implying his own individual essence, no one knows any propositions implying the individual essence of anyone else.' Notice that Chisholm qualifies the knowledge we have of our own essences as *direct* and *immediate*. He then claims that no one can know a proposition implying the individual essence of anyone else; but why not include the qualifiers here as well? With the qualifiers in place, we get the following account of self-awareness:

SA3: S has self-awareness of R $=_{df.}$ (i) S directly and immediately believes that p, and (ii) p implies the individual essence of R.

The revised corollary could then be stated as:

COR2: No one directly and immediately grasps the individual essence of any other thing.

Given SA3 and COR2, it does not follow that no one can know or grasp a proposition implying the individual essence of any other thing; all that follows is that no one can directly and immediately know, directly and immediately grasp a proposition implying the individual essence of anything else.

The avenue of escape which SA3 and COR2 supplies for the propositional theory requires taking belief (and perhaps other intentional states as well) to be a triadic relation rather than, as Chisholm holds, a dyadic relation. The reason the problem of private propositions arose for Chisholm is because on his view, there are only two components to belief: the particular intentional attitude, namely, believing, and the object of that attitude, namely, a proposition. On a view which includes SA3 and COR2, there are three components to belief: the particular intentional attitude, the object of belief, and *the way in which the propositional object is accessed.* We shall have more to say about triadic theories of belief in the next section, but for now at least this much is clear. SA3 and COR2 together undermine the first argument that COR1 is a corollary of a propositional theory of *de se* awareness. One of the premises of the argument for COR1 which I put in Chisholm's mouth was that an adequate account of self-awareness must be supplemented by COR1. I submit that SA3 with COR2 gives an alternative, one which does not imply COR1; hence the first argument should not convince us to accept COR1.

This first argument does not exhaust the possible arguments for COR1, though; hence, in order to justifiably reject that COR1 is an accompaniment to any propositional theory, we must examine other arguments which might be used to show that COR1 is a corollary of that theory. There are two other arguments of which I am aware for the claim that COR1 is a corollary.[40] The first arises from Chisholm's view that the only object that can be individuated *per se* is oneself and that any other sort of individuation that occurs, occurs in virtue of some relation that obtains between the individuated object and what can be individuated *per se*.[41] Now, if both these claims are true, it follows that the proposition that one accepts in individuating oneself is a proposition that no one else could access, for if they had access to that very same proposition, they would be individuating someone other than themselves *per se*. But, by hypothesis, each of us can only individuate himself *per se*, so there must be private propositions.

This argument is bad on several counts. First, it proves too much. It not only follows that propositions about ourselves are private, all propositions including any sort of individuation (*per se* or not) will be private, if the type of individuation is an essential part of the proposition in question (as the argument above assumed). Consider any object which is individuated. By the hypothesis above, it is individuated only by some relation that obtains between the individuated object and what can be individuated *per se*. Since what is individuated *per se* is my essence, anything else that is individuated by me is individuated by some relation that object bears to my essence. So, any proposition accepted which includes this sort of individuation will be infected with my essence (assuming again that the type of individuation employed "infects" any proposition at all); and since no one has access to my essence but me, no one can have access to any proposition which includes this sort of individuation but me.

Second, it is not clear that individuation *per se* is possible only with regard to oneself. It is clearly not indefensible to suggest that one can refer to an object directly, and hence individuate it *per se*, without referring to it only by virtue of some individuating description. Our earlier example from our discussion of the reducibility of *de re* beliefs to *de dicto* may be an example of this sort: the four-year-old believing what is expressed by the sentence 'that ball is yellow'.

Third, the argument does not prove enough. It does not prove that private propositions are required since we can use the same notion of direct grasping or believing here as we did before to undermine the first argument for the privacy view. Even if individuation *per se* can only occur with respect to oneself, this at best shows that one can grasp some propositions in an especially direct and immediate way which no one but oneself can. It does not show that there is a special content of one's belief that no one else can access. Hence, this argument fares no better than the first.

There is one more argument to evaluate. Consider Hume's belief expressed by the sentence 'I'm Hume'. Now, consider Heimsohn trying to believe exactly what Hume believes. Can he believe what Hume believes by believing what is expressed for him by his use of the sentence 'I'm Hume'? Of course not, for what Hume believes is true, and what Heimsohn would believe if he believed what is expressed by that sentence is false.

The natural attempt here is for Heimsohn to believe what is

expressed by the sentence 'He's Hume'. Some, though, would claim that this belief could not be the same as Hume's belief, for if two persons are in identical total mental states it is at least highly probable (if not entailed) that their behaviour is the same. So suppose we grant that Hume and Heimsohn have exactly the same mental constitution except for their beliefs about who is who. Hume believes what is expressed by the sentence 'I am Hume and he is not', and Heimsohn believes what is expressed by the sentence 'He is Hume and I am not'. If we accept that they are believing the same proposition, and also hold that their attitude towards that proposition (the attitude of believing) is the same, then Hume and Heimsohn are in identical total mental states. Yet it is totally improbable that their behaviour is the same. Should they both acquire the belief that Hume is being called to the front of the room, only Hume would go; Heimsohn would not. Hence, if we claim their beliefs are the same, we have no explanation of the difference in their behaviour on the basis of their individual mental states and in particular, the principle which claims that behaviour is the same, if mental states are the same, is violated.

If we accept SA1 as the proper account of self-awareness, this argument, if sound, would give a good reason to supplement SA1 with COR1. However, even if we grant the crucial principle of the argument (that if two persons are in identical total mental states, then their behaviour is the same (all else being equal)), SA3 with COR2 handles this case just as well, for they imply that though Hume and Heimsohn are believing the same proposition, they are not believing it in the same way. Hume is directly and immediately grasping a proposition which implies his own individual essence; Heimsohn is not. Hence, there is no need to expect their behaviour to be the same.

I conclude then that there is no need for the propositional theory to accept COR1. Further, since there is good reason to reject COR1, I am convinced that the propositional account of *de se* awareness, in its most plausible form, should not affirm the existence of private propositions.

We saw earlier that Chisholm's rejecting the old theory and presenting the new property theory involves two distinct features. The first is abandoning the propositional view, and the second is positing an order of explanation from self-awareness to other-awareness. We found reason to reject his theory, in particular because of the latter of the two characteristics just mentioned; we are now in a position to see that there is no good reason for rejecting the propositional view either. The only reason we could discover for abandoning the propositional view in favour of a property view was that the propositional view seemed committed to private propositions. We have seen, though, that such is not the case. Hence there is no good reason for abandoning the intuitively plausible propositional view in favour of a possible view, the only developed version of which is clearly inadequate.

Further, notice that the sort of problem which undermined Chisholm's view – namely, being unable to distinguish in certain cases an impossible state of affairs from one which cannot be truly believed not to obtain – does not arise for a propositional theory that distinguishes between direct and indirect grasping. When I consider my own non-existence, I directly grasp a proposition which implies my non-existence; there is nothing paradoxical about such a thought. There would be a problem if we accepted the view that there are special sorts of first-person propositions which are contingent entities, as Castaneda does, for then the same inability to distinguish impossible states of affairs from those that merely imply one's own non-existence arises. To see this, suppose one is considering the possibility that oneself does not exist. That claim is identical to the claim that there is a world in which it is false that one exists. Yet, if propositions about oneself are contingent, it is impossible that there be such a world since there are no worlds in which there is a proposition about one's existence which is false. This argument gives us a good reason to reject the view that there are first-person propositions which are contingent entities. So, by accepting the distinction between direct and indirect grasping and by refusing to posit contingent first-person propositions, we can avoid both the problem for Chisholm's property theory and the purported problem of private propositions for the propositional view of the objects of intentional attitudes.

A New Propositional Theory

We need then to clarify this new propositional theory. The theory begins by affirming principles (6)–(9) given earlier concerning the nature of propositions: propositions are necessary beings composed of properties which are bearers of truth-values. Further, the contents of the intentional attitudes of believing and knowing are propositions; though I think the contents of all intentional attitudes are propositions, the purpose of this work does not require a defence of that view. Hence I shall only claim that the attitudes of believing and knowing are directed towards propositions.

The heart of this theory, it will be remembered, involves the claim that belief is a triadic relation between an intentional attitude, a proposition, and a particular manner of accessing the proposition. The particular feature of the theory that enables us to avoid the problem of private propositions is the distinction between direct and indirect grasping. Though some revision of the following account will be called for later, our present concerns can be met by these principles:

P3: For all x and y, if x either directly or indirectly grasps y, then y is a proposition.

P4: For all x and y, if x directly graps y, then y includes x's essence.

P5: For all intentional attitudes of believing or knowing, A, A includes grasping (either directly or indirectly) as an essential part.

P6: For all x, y, and z, if x directly graps y, then y is necessarily such that, for all z such that z is non-identical to x, z does not directly grasp y.

These principles employ certain terms that stand in need of clarification. The definitions of the terms are:

D9: Property P is an essence of $x =_{df.} P$ is necessarily such that (i) it is possible that something exemplify it; (ii) it is not possible that anything other than x exemplify it; and (iii) it is not possible that x exist and not exemplify it.

D10: Intentional attitude A includes e as an essential part $=_{df.} A$ is necessarily such that if it obtains, it has e as a part.

D11: Proposition p includes property $R =_{df.} p$ is necessarily such that whoever conceives it, conceives R.

These principles and definitions leave unanswered the question whether we should accept a propositional theory which is a reductive or non-reductive. A *reductive theory* would attempt to define *de dicto* and *de re* belief in terms of the notion of direct grasping, which in turn would be the essential notion in defining *de se* belief. Alternatively, a *non-reductive theory* would define *de dicto* belief in terms of indirect grasping, making no attempt to reduce indirect grasping to some collection of direct graspings. In addition, subtypes of non-reductive theories emerge in relation to the issue of how to clarify *de re* belief. A *fully non-reductive theory* would claim that some *de re* beliefs cannot be captured by any sort of grasping of a proposition, direct or indirect. A *partially non-reductive theory* would claim that the cognitive content of a *de re* belief can be captured by some sort of grasping of a proposition, though no such grasping insures that that there is the right sort of epistemic intimacy to the object in question necessary for *de re* belief. A *minimally non-reductive theory* would claim, as above, that indirect grasping cannot be clarified by direct grasping, though *de re* belief can be fully reduced to some collection of direct and indirect graspings. Finally, a *substantially non-reductive theory* would claim that indirect grasping can be reduced to direct grasping, but *de re* belief cannot be reduced to either. Depending on the type of non-reducibility that such a substantially non-reductive theory claims, we may have either a *partially and substantially non-reductive theory* (one which allows that the cognitive content of a *de re* belief is to be clarified in terms of that which is directly or indirectly grasped, though such a cognitive content does not guarantee the proper sort of epistemic intimacy needed for *de re* belief) or a *fully and substantially non-reductive theory* (which claims that neither the cognitive content nor the epistemic intimacy constitutive of *de re* belief can be captured by a collection of direct and indirect graspings).

These issues deserve full and careful exploration, but they are quite beyond the scope of this work. My point here is only to show that, though it initially appears that the traditional account of omniscience is wedded to a reductive account of the objects of intentional attitudes on which any sort of awareness is reduced to *de dicto* awareness, this appearance is far from true. On the contrary, there is no reason to think that even a fully and substantially non-reductive theory is incompatible with the traditional account of omniscience. Yet, since it is not necessary to sort out whether a reductive or non-reductive version of the propositional theory above is correct for the purposes of this work, I shall leave the issues involved for another time.

A different question which we ought not to pass over concerns the ground of the distinction between direct and indirect grasping. I have claimed that there is a fundamental distinction between two ways of accessing propositions, yet not much light has been thrown on this claim by the distinction above. We want to know in addition what this talk of ways of accessing propositions comes to.

If we consider again the Hume–Heimsohn case discussed earlier, we may shed some light on this question. I claimed, regarding that case, that when Hume believes what is expressed by the sentence 'I'm Hume', he is believing the same proposition that Heimsohn believes when he believes what is expressed by the sentence 'He's Hume'. None the less, the way in which each accesses the proposition in question is different.

How so? A natural response here is that the propositions are accessed *through* the meanings of the sentences in question.

For such a response to be acceptable, we must deny the view that the meanings of the words 'he' and 'I' are purely referential; for, if they were, then the meanings of the two sentences would be identical. Such a denial is quite plausible, though, if one accepts this sort of triadic theory of belief. If such terms are purely referential and this theory of belief is accepted, then one will have no explanation of the difference between noting that one's own pants are on fire (by believing what is expressed by 'my pants are on fire') and merely noting that the person in the mirror (who happens to be oneself) has pants which are on fire (by believing what is expressed by 'his pants are on fire'). The only way to explain this case and hold that 'he' and 'I' are purely referential is to hold that the reference of 'I' is different from any possible reference of 'he'. Thus, rather than posit private propositions, such a view is committed to private meanings by virtue of being committed to a reference for any first-person pronoun to which no second- or third-person pronoun could refer.

A theory including private meanings is as objectionable as one including private propositions. When my wife says, 'I have a dental appointment today', I cannot only literally and truthfully claim to know the proposition she expressed, I can also literally and truthfully claim to know what she means. In order to override such obvious intuitions, we need strong arguments; and, as far as I can see, there are none forthcoming.

Happily, positing private meanings is not the only alternative, even if one wishes to hold that the force of pronouns is substantially referential. One might say, for example, that the meaning of a third-person pronoun is *a thing demonstrated* (because a demonstration is needed to secure the reference) and the meaning of a second-person pronoun is *a thing addressed* (because a use of such a pronoun requires a form of addressing). Finally, the meaning of a first-person pronoun is the speaker or writer in question who, if demonstrated or addressed, need not be.[42]

Another alternative is to take the meaning of such terms in such a way that each normal use of 'he' has the same meaning, as does 'I'. One might say that the meaning of such terms is the cognitive content of the term. Therefore, when I say 'I'm tired', I mean the same thing you mean when you utter those words.

In either case, the meaning of the sentences used which express the proposition in question provides an explanation for the distinction between direct and indirect grasping. In the referential view, the reference to oneself has a sort of immediacy about it which no other reference has (because any other reference requires either a form of addressing or a form of demonstrating). In the second view, the meaning of any first-person sentence is not equivalent to the meaning of any second- or third-person sentence. Hence, the way in which a proposition about oneself (as oneself) is accessed is distinct from the way in which a proposition about anyone else is accessed.

What we have seen, then, is that the propositional theory can avoid the problem of private propositions by rejecting a dyadic propositional theory in favour of a triadic propositional theory. The third *relatum*, I have suggested, is the meaning of the sentence used to express the proposition in question. Such a view explains the distinction I have posited between direct and indirect grasping of propositions.

Kinds of Belief and Omniscience

It is now time to draw the implications of this study of belief and its contents for the standard construal of omniscience is captured in principle O. It may seem that the answer is obvious. The point has been to show that O is not undermined by consideration concerning *de re* and *de se* attitudes, and that has been accomplished (or so I claim).

Things are not quite so obvious, though, for even if all I have said is correct, a being could know all truths and yet fail to be maximally excellent with regard to his awareness of all there is. Suppose, for example, that a being knew all there is to know about himself, but never in such a way that he directly grasps his own essence. Such a being, even if he knew every truth about himself, would not know himself *as himself*, and thus would be cognitively inferior to any being that did know every truth about himself, as well as knowing himself as himself.

We are thus faced with two options. Either we can clarify omniscience as O does and note that being omniscient does not exhaust the cognitive excellence of God (for, since God is maximally perfect, he also exhibits maximal cognitive excellence), or we can include the notion of maximal cognitive excellence in the notion of omniscience itself.

The first course, I think, is preferable. I am not positive that the concept of omniscience does not include the concept of maximal cognitive excellence; however, it is clear that the concept of knowledge itself does not include the property of exhibiting cognitive perfection, even concerning the area of inquiry in question.[43] We can know even though our cognitive functioning is quite deficient even from our own point of view, hence having knowledge is distinct from exhibiting cognitive excellences. Though this argument does not entail that omniscience does not include the concept of maximal cognitive excellence, since I cannot see any reason for thinking that omniscience does include maximal cognitive excellence, I take the fact that knowledge does not require cognitive excellence as evidence that we should not clarify omniscience to require it. Hence I conclude that we ought to accept O, but that O by itself does not fully specify the cognitive excellences of God.

CONCLUSION

The implication of the above discussion for the doctrine of omniscience is that we can accept the exceedingly simple formulation offered earlier. A being is omniscient if and only if that being believes all and only what is true, and justifiably believes all and only what he believes. Such a being need not be able to grasp directly all of what he believes; for most propositions that will be a logically impossible task. Since grasping is a type of mental act, it will be relevant to the doctrine of omnipotence, not omniscience. And, since grasping directly all of what an omniscient being believes is a logically impossible task, such a being need not be able to perform such tasks in order to be omnipotent. Thus I conclude that the problem of *de re* and *de se* attitudes is surmountable; the doctrine of omniscience does not require revision in the face of these different attitudes.

We turn then to the objections that have been formulated against the doctrine of omniscience; in particular, to the objection that God's knowing the future is incompatible with human actions being done freely.

3 God's Certainty and Man's Freedom

INTRODUCTION

Philosophers have long worried that holding to the doctrine that God is omniscient is incompatible with human beings having freedom of the sort that is anti-deterministic.[1] *Prima facie*, they are wrong: knowledge does not, by its mere existence, make true what is known, rather it is truth that makes knowledge possible. But many have not been impressed with this simple response and have thought that there is something special about God's knowledge which shows that this simple response is quite misleading, and which results in an incompatibility between divine omniscience and human freedom.

The suspicion that there is such an incompatibility has led to various attempts to formulate arguments intended to support the thesis that God's foreknowledge is incompatible with human freedom. We can find such a formulation of the problem at least as early as Augustine. He says:

> Your trouble is this. You wonder how it can be that these two propositions are not contradictory and incompatible, namely that God has foreknowledge of all future events, and that we sin voluntarily and not by necessity. For if, you say, God foreknows that a man will sin, he must necessarily sin. But if there is necessity there is no voluntary choice of sinning, but rather fixed and unavoidable necessity.[2]

One way to miss the force of this objection is to confuse the problem of the compatibility between divine foreknowledge and human freedom with the compatibility between foreknowledge and human freedom. This confusion shows itself in the following sort of response to the objection we are considering: since one person can know in advance what another will do without endangering the freedom of that other person, just so, God can know what we will do without endangering

72

our freedom. Frederick Schleiermacher takes exactly this line of defence against the incompatibility thesis. He says:

> In the same way, we estimate the intimacy between two persons by the foreknowledge one has of the actions of the other, without supposing that in either case, the one or the other's freedom is thereby endangered. So even the divine foreknowledge cannot endanger freedom.[3]

And Augustine makes the same point in *De Libero Arbitrio*:

> Unless I am mistaken, you would not directly compel the man to sin, though you knew beforehand that he was going to sin. Nor does your prescience in itself compel him to sin even though he was certainly going to sin, as we must assume if you have real prescience. So there is no contradiction here. Simply you know beforehand what another is going to do with his own will. Similarly God compels no man to sin, though he sees beforehand those who are going to sin by their own will.[4]

In spite of the attractiveness of this sort of response, it is inadequate because it confuses the problem of foreknowledge with the problem of divine foreknowledge. To see that these problems are different, we need only note the difference between God's knowledge and ours. To say that a being is omniscient is not to posit any kind of knowledge different from our own, except with regard to the extent of that knowledge; however, we have also seen that God's knowledge is not only more extensive than ours, its very nature is different because God is not only omniscient, He is essentially omniscient. As we saw in Chapter 1, to claim that God is essentially omniscient implies that God is absolutely certain about everything which He believes. And that certainty entails that God bears a very different relation to the future than we do, for we cannot be certain in the relevant sense of much more than our own present mental states.

Thus, whatever there is to be said regarding the incompatibility thesis, the thesis that God's foreknowledge is incompatible with human freedom, it cannot be dismissed by considering the case of ordinary foreknowledge – which is quite unlike God's foreknowledge.

None the less, noting this disanalogy does not imply that God's foreknowledge is incompatible with human freedom. Perhaps the analogy is not a decisive one because of the difference between God's foreknowledge and ours, but that point merely shows that the compatibilist's position – the position which claims that God's foreknowledge is compatible with human freedom – has not yet been successfully defended. So, noting the disanalogy can at best show that the issue between compatibilists and incompatibilists – those that defend the incompatibility theses – has not yet been settled.

One difficulty surrounding the discussion of the incompatibility thesis is that the normal statements of the issue mask several different arguments under one formulation. The initial formulation (Augustine's), with its emphasis on anti-deterministic freedom, might suggest that the objector is thinking that God's foreknowledge *causes* what he foreknows. I shall examine this form of the argument first; though, as we shall see, it is far from the most imposing argument for the incompatibility thesis. There are two other arguments besides the causal argument, one centring on certain features of the future, the other centring on certain features about the past. These arguments, especially the latter, are much more imposing than the first; but, lest we get ahead of ourselves, let us turn first to the causal argument for the incompatibility thesis.

CERTAINTY, CAUSALITY AND FREEDOM

As I pointed out above, the causal version of the incompatibility thesis arises from considering the nature of God's knowledge. For not only is God's knowledge more extensive than ours, it is of a different kind as well (assuming, of course, that the doctrine of essential omniscience is defensible – an assumption which I shall make here and defend later). Whereas we have come to realise that humans can still be knowers even though our justification is fallible, God's knowledge is infallible. And to say that God's knowledge is infallible is to say more than the trivial truth that if God knows *p*, *p* is true. It is to say that God couldn't be mistaken, it is to say something about God's nature, rather than knowledge itself. If God believes a proposition, that by itself guarantees that that proposition is true, for God does not make mistakes about what to believe and what not to as we do. Further, he has the property of essentially not making mistakes, he simply could not make a mistake about what to believe and what not to. Thus, there is a sense in which God's knowledge is characterised by absolute certainty, whereas our knowledge is not.

We saw in Chapter 2 the sort of notion of absolute certainty that we are considering. It is:

AC: p is absolutely certain for $S =_{df.} p$ is true; if S were to believe p, p would be true; and if S were to fail to believe p, then *not-p* would be true.

In order for God's certainty to be a reason for accepting the incompatibility thesis, there must be some connection between the concept of certainty and the concept of causality. I shall begin by first attempting to motivate a certain view of causality, the view that makes the strongest causal argument for the incompatibility thesis. After motivating this view of causality, I shall show the connections between this view of causality and the absolute certainty of God's knowledge. We shall then be in a position to evaluate the strength of the argument.

Causality

Suppose we encounter someone who is uncertain what the word 'cause' means. Natural explanations would include such locutions as 'bringing about', 'depends on', etc. We might say that for one thing to cause another is for the first to bring about some change or lack of change in another, or we might say that the occurrence of the second depends on the occurrence of the first. But what does it mean for one thing to depend on another? One is naturally led to utter, with Hume, certain conditionals: if the first occurs, so will the second; or if the first hadn't occurred, neither would the second.[5]

Thus, it would seem that if causality is analysable at all, it is to be analysed in terms of conditional statements. But what sorts of conditionals? We have several options. First, we might try the standard material conditional. Such an approach, though, has the difficulty of being too weak to account for a causal connection. To say that c causes e entails that both e and c occur; and this conjunctive occurrence by itself entails that the occurrence of c is both materially necessary and sufficient for the occurrence of e. But certainly the fact that both c and e occur does not entail that either is a cause of the other.

The standard attempt to handle this problem is to make the material conditional hold between event-types, rather than event-tokens.[6] But no specification of which types count and which do not seems forthcoming. And since for any two event-tokens, there is some type of which they are tokens for which the conditionality relation holds, we would perhaps be justified in looking for another explication of the sort of conditional we are to use in giving a conditional analysis of causation.[7]

Perhaps we could try a strict implication interpretation instead. This approach, however, has the opposite problem: it seems too strong to be the causal relation. To say that *c* causes *e* does not imply that it is logically impossible that *c* occur and *e* not occur.

One way to attempt to avoid this problem is to construe the implication as holding, not between *c* and *e* alone, but rather between the laws of nature $L_1 \ldots L_n$, some set of initial conditions $C_1 \ldots C_n$ (which include the occurrence of *c*), and *e*.[8] Thus, to say that *c* is a cause of *e* is to say that $L_1 \ldots L_n$ and $C_1 \ldots C_n$ strictly imply that *e* occurs.

But, though this attempt does avoid some problems, there is another perhaps more difficult problem with the strict implication approach. If there is an entailment relation between the laws in question, the set of initial conditions, and *e*, there is also such an entailment relation between those same laws, some other set of initial conditions which include *not-e*, and *not-c*. For, if the conjunction between the laws of nature and the initial conditions which include the occurrence of *c* entails the occurrence of *e*, there will also be an entailment relation between those same laws, a set of conditions just like the first except where *c* is replaced by the non-occurrence of *e* (and what these changes entail), and *not-c*. What I am claiming is that, if we can get the required entailment relation for *c* to be a cause of *e*, we can also get the required entailment relation so that *not-e* would be a cause of *not-c*. But then we are forced to say that if a certain rattlesnake bite causes the death of some individual, were that individual not to have died, that event would have caused it to be the case that the rattlesnake did not bite that individual. Such an implication shows severe problems for the strict entailment interpretation of causal statements.

So, it would seem, there is some reason at least to look for another sort of conditional other than the two considered above. And there is one ready at hand which has some of the virtues the lack of which undermined the analyses employing the other sorts of conditionals. It is the conditional standardly expressed using the subjunctive mood: if I were to hit you, you would be angry. Such conditionals are distinctive in that their truth value does not depend on the truth-value of the indicative utterance of the antecedent alone. In the example I just used, its truth is independent of the truth of the proposition *I hit you*. Such conditionals seem to be just the sort we are looking for. They are stronger than material conditionals, as can be seen by noting that the falsity of the antecedent does not guarantee the truth of the whole statement. And they are weaker conditionals than those involving strict implication: the truth of the earlier statement does not mean that my hitting you would logically preclude a quite placid response on your part. Further, we cannot perform the transposition operating on conditionals of this sort (at least not on the standard Lewis–Stalnaker semantics for such conditionals):[9] from 'if c were to occur, e would' we cannot infer 'if e were to fail to occur, c would fail to occur as well'. So, if there is a way to employ such conditionals in analysing causation, we need not face the earlier problem that the absence of the effect would be a cause of the absence of a cause. Finally, there is a sort of natural attraction to such an account of causation; for as we noted earlier, when prompted concerning the nature of causation, we are naturally led to utter conditionals of this sort. We say things like, 'c is a cause of e means that if c occurs, so would e; and if c didn't occur, e wouldn't either'.[10] Thus, perhaps in this sort of conditional we find hope for an adequate conditional analysis of causation. Hereafter I shall refer to this kind of conditional as a counterfactual conditional.

Certainty and Causality

But what connection is there between this sort of analysis of causation and God's knowledge? If we consider AC again, we can see that this concept of certainty is closely connected with the sort of conditionals which seemed the most plausible candidates for an analysis of causation. Now we have not clarified God's certainty in precisely this fashion, for we have clarified God's certainty by the following claim: necessarily, God believes that p if and only if p is true. But, even if the conditionals in this claim are only material conditionals, there are plausible assumptions under which our clarification of God's certainty implies the sort of absolute certainty defined in AC. These assumptions are simply those of the standard possible worlds semantics both for necessity claims in general and for counterfactual claims. To say that p *only if q* is necessarily true is to say that q is true in every world in which p is; and to say that p counterfactually implies q is to say that any world in which both p and q are true is a world closer (on relevant grounds of similarity) to the actual world than any world in which p is true and q is false.

The inference is now obvious. Our definition of God's certainty implies that *God believes that p* is true in every world in which p is true.

Now, either God believes that p in no worlds or in some worlds. If God believes that p in no worlds, then both counterfactuals *if God believes that p, then p* and *if God fails to believe that p, then not p* are vacuously true simply because there is no possible world in which either antecedent is true. So consider the other alternative, that God believes that p in some worlds. Call this set of worlds W. On the standard semantics, to say that if God were to believe that p then p, is to make a claim about a subclass of this set W: that any world where p is false is a world farther from the actual world than one in which p is true. But, by hypothesis, p is true in every member of W, and thus the counterfactual claim is true. And the same argument works for the other counterfactual in question – that if God were to fail to believe that p, then not-p. That God fails to believe that p is true in some set of worlds W', and the counterfactual claim requires that p be false in some subset of W'. But since that proposition is false in every member of W' by hypothesis, it follows that it is false in the required subset of W'.

All of this comes to the following. Our understanding of essential omniscience entails that if God were to believe that p, then p; and if God were to fail to believe that p, then not-p. But this conjunction is exactly of the sort that would be an appropriate place to look for a counterfactual analysis of causality; in fact, it is roughly equivalent to David Lewis's counterfactual analysis. According to Lewis:

> C: c is a cause of e =$_{df.}$ there is an ordered series of events $c_1 \ldots c_n$ of which c is a member such that c_2 causally depends on c_1, c_3 on $c_2 \ldots$, c_n on c_{n-1}, and e on c_n.[11]

The critical concept in this definition is the notion of causal dependence, and Lewis clarifies it by the counterfactual conditionals we have been discussing. He claims:

> CD: e is causally dependent on c =$_{df.}$ (i) if c were to occur, e would occur, and (ii) if c were to fail to occur, e would fail to occur.[12]

We have then an implication from the nature of God's certainty to the infallibilists' notion of absolute certainty, and at least a plausible theory of causation on which there is an implication from absolute certainty to causality. Thus if any S is absolutely certain that p, S's being absolutely certain that p is a cause of the truth of the proposition that p. So if God is essentially omniscient, He is responsible for the truth of that which He knows. And thus, in particular, He is responsible for which actions human beings perform; and His being so responsible is incompatible with these actions being anti-deterministic-ally free.

The Failure of the Argument

The failure of this argument is to be found by examining more carefully Lewis's counterfactual analysis of causality, which is not free of difficulties. Some of the problems with his analysis can be handled by taking care in understanding what counts as an event. I am assuming here that causal relations are relations between events, so we must at least allow that an event is either a change or lack of change in an object since both changes and lacks of changes have effects. But if this is all we have to say about events, the counterfactual theory implies that every mathematical truth is a cause of every other. Since both *two's equalling one plus one* and *three's equalling two plus one* involve lacks of changes in objects, both count as events on the above understanding of events. But if two were to equal one plus one, three would equal two plus one; and if two were to fail to equal one plus one, three would fail to equal two plus one. Then, on Lewis's definitions, *three's equalling two plus one* is causally dependent on, and hence is caused by, *two's equalling one plus one*.

We can avoid this problem by altering our understanding of events. We should say, I think, that an event is a change or lack of change in an object that comes to an end at some time. Then, *two's equalling one plus one* is not an event, and thus cannot be a cause of, or caused by, anything.

But even if we agree on this understanding of events, problems remain; for *today's being Friday* is an event and so is *tomorrow's being Saturday*.[13] Further, the occurrence of the first event entails the second; and we have already seen that if such entailment relation holds, the counterfactual claims involved in the counterfactual analysis of causation are true. But it would be wrong to say that *today's being Friday* is a cause of *tomorrow's being Saturday*; hence the counterfactual theory has the problem of confusing logical and causal relations.

There is a characteristic of the two events above that may help in developing a plausible version of the counterfactual analysis of causation. The characteristic is that the logical relation between the two events is symmetrical. But causal relations are asymmetrical; if *c* is a cause of *e*, then *e* is not a cause of *c*.

Capturing the asymmetry requirement is one of the most serious difficulties for the counterfactual theory of causality. The problem is that for many cases in which the counterfactuals required by CD are true, the corresponding counterfactuals in which e and c exchange places are also true. One way to attempt to capture this requirement is to replace CD by:

CD′: e is causally dependent on $c =_{df.}$ (i) if c were to occur, so would e; (ii) if c were to fail to occur, so would e; and (iii) condition (i) or (ii) would be false where 'c' and 'e' exchange places.

This alteration allows us to avoid the problematic implication that *today's being Friday* is a cause of *tomorrow's being Saturday*, for the first two conditions are true regardless of which event comes first in the conditionals, and so these two events violate clause (iii) of the above definition. However, it has other problems, for there are cases in which it still appears to violate the asymmetry requirement. For example, suppose I turn on the light by flipping a switch. There are many complicated events which intervene between those two, but let us simplify by letting b be the conjunction of them all. Then our definitions imply that my turning on the light is caused by my flipping the switch, for the following counterfactuals are true:

(CF1) if I were to flip the switch b would occur, and if b were to occur the light would come on; and if I were not to flip the switch b would not occur, and if b would not occur the light would not come on.

However, the reverse counterfactuals seem to be true as well:

(CF2) if the light were to fail to come on b would have failed to occur, and if b had failed to occur I would not have flipped the switch; and if the light came on, b would have occurred, and if b occurred I would have flipped the switch.

Thus, CD′ seems to be too strong: it preserves the asymmetry requirement only by sacrificing some obvious causal relations between events.

The recent attempts to avoid this problem arise in the context of giving a possible worlds semantics for counterfactuals. Such a semantics takes as primitive the notion of similarity between possible worlds, and then claims that a counterfactual relation from A to B is true just in case, for any A world in which B is not true, there is a world closer to the actual world in which both A and B are true. One attempt to avoid the above sort of problem is to explain the relation of similarity, or closeness, between possible worlds in such a way that (CFl) comes out true and (CF2) comes out false. Alternatively, one might simply grant that both (CF1) and (CF2) are true, and then abandon CD' and argue that certain characteristics of the worlds under discussion bars the set of counterfactuals in (CF2) from signalling a causal relation.

The first route, taken by Lewis, allows that we can consider worlds in which miracles (violations of laws of nature) take place in determining whether the counterfactuals are true or not. Since it would only take a small miracle for *b* to occur and for the lights to have failed to come on, one might suggest that this shows that (CF2) is false.[14] Why? Because a world in which a small miracle occurs is more similar to the actual world than a world in which that miracle does not occur. The reason for this is that if determinism is true, then for a certain event not to occur which has occurred requires that the entire history of the world be different. Thus, in the case at hand, if the lights hadn't come on and the switch was not flipped, then the whole history of that world would have been different from the history of the actual world. However, if a small miracle were to occur, a world could have exactly the same history as this one and yet be one in which the switch is flipped and the light does not come on. Hence, on grounds of similarity, one might argue that the most similar worlds are such that (CF2) is false, so that we have no counter-example to the theory of causality presented earlier which includes CD'.

Swain, on the other hand, suggests that both (CF1) and (CF2) are true, but that there are characteristics of the worlds in question on which we can prefer (CF1) as the signaller of causality to (CF2). He suggests that one look at the closest worlds in which *c* occurs and *e* does not, and in which *e* occurs but *c* does not. For *c* to be a cause of *e*, assuming mutual causal dependence as defined by CD (as in (CF1) and (CF2)), the following conditions must hold regarding those worlds: for *e* not to have occurred when *c* does, such a world would only have to lack some event *a* (other than *c*) upon which *e* also causally depends; and for *c* not to have occurred where *e* does occur, such a world would have to fail to include some event *f* upon which *c* causally depends, and such a world would have had to include some other event *g* upon which *e* is causally dependent, though not so dependent in the actual world. The intuition here is that, when *c* is a cause of *e*, a mere prevention could make the counterfactual from *c* to *e* false; whereas for the counterfactual from *e* to *c* to be false requires the absence of some cause of *c* as well as the presence of something which did not cause *e*. In the light bulb case above, it is plausible to think that this condition is satisfied. It would only take a prevention to keep the light from coming on when the switch is flipped, but it would take both the absence of some cause of the switch's being flipped as well as the presence of some additional element to bring about the coming on of the light. Hence, according to Swain's theory, the causal relation goes only from the flip of the switch to the coming on of the light.[15]

My intention here is not to solve the problems for the counterfactual theory, for I am not sure they can be; in fact, I am not sure that causation is analysable. What I am attempting is, first, to show the connection between the incompatibility thesis and the counterfactual theory of causality, and, second, to show that the connection is not one which can establish the incompatibility thesis. In particular, I am defending the claim that one step on the road to an adequate counterfactual analysis must include the restrictions on events I have specified (or, of course, some other ontology with the same implications as the restrictions I have imposed) and some way of accounting for the asymmetric character of causality.

If I am right about this, then there is sufficient reason to dismiss this argument for the incompatibility thesis, for the implication from certainty to causality disappears. In the case of God's certainty, there is a mutual entailment relation between what God believes and the truth of what he believes. Hence there are no possible worlds grounds for distinguishing one counterfactual dependency from the other, and hence the asymmetry requirement is violated in the case of God's being certain and that of which He is certain. Perhaps there is some way other than through possible worlds to prefer one direction of counterfactual dependency to another, but if there is, it is not obvious. There is thus good reason to find the causal argument for the incompatibility thesis less than satisfactory.

Further, *God's believing that p* does not count as an event on the criterion I am employing. In fact, even *God's coming to believe that p* is not normally an event. Perhaps for most persons coming to believe a certain claim is normally an event, but not for God. He does not generally come to believe any truth, rather He has always believed that a claim is true if it in fact is.

So there is no causal incompatibility between God's foreknowledge and human freedom; if the incompatibility thesis is to be defended, such a defence will have to be found elsewhere. There are attempts of this sort, one centring on features of the future and the other centring on features of the past. We turn first to the grounding of the incompatibility thesis on the features of the future.

FATALISM AND FREEDOM

Boethius formulates the problem of foreknowledge and freedom as follows:

> There seems to be a hopeless conflict between divine foreknowledge of all things and freedom of the human will. For if God sees everything in advance and cannot be deceived in any way, whatever his Providence foresees will happen, must happen. Therefore, if God foreknows eternally not only all the acts of men, but also their plans and wishes, there cannot be freedom of will; for nothing whatever can be done or even desired without its being known beforehand by the infallible Providence of God. If things could somehow be accomplished in some way other than that which God foresaw, his foreknowledge of the future would no longer be certain. Indeed, it would be merely uncertain opinion, and it would be wrong to think that of God.[16]

Boethius took this to be a quite different problem from the issue raised by the causal argument we considered in the last section, for he goes on to claim,

> I cannot agree with the argument by which some people believe that they can solve this problem. They say that things do not happen because Providence foresees that they will happen, but, on the contrary, that Providence foresees what is to come because it will happen, and in this way they find the necessity to be in things, not in Providence. For, they say, it is not necessary that things should happen because they are foreseen, but only that things which will happen be foreseen – as though the problem were whether divine Providence is the cause of the necessity of future events, or the necessity of future events is the cause of divine Providence. But our concern is to prove that the fulfilment of things which God has foreseen is necessary, whatever the order of causes, even if the divine foreknowledge does not seem to make the occurrence of future events necessary.[17]

Boethius recognises the asymmetry requirement for causal statements, and considers the reply that his problem is solved by noting that the causal relation goes from things to God rather than from God's providence to things. Boethius just as clearly rejects this answer; as he claims, 'our concern is (not with) the order of causes'. Thus, the argument suggested by Boethius cannot be dismissed as an instance of the type of argument we rejected in the last section; the sort of necessity it discusses is not causal necessity. The sort of necessity under consideration is not clear from the passages quoted, but one interpretation might be that the sort of necessity in question is a logical or metaphysical sort; on this interpretation, Boethius' worry would be that it is logically necessary that what God has foreseen comes about, and that the existence of this necessity is incompatible with what is foreseen being truly free. Thus, whereas we could call the argument of the preceding section an argument for theological determinism, we would call the argument resulting from this interpretation of the passages above an argument for theological fatalism.

Theological fatalism bears very close relations to ordinary fatalism. Consider Taylor's provoking story of an Indian resident named Osmo. As it turns out, quite a few years before Osmo's birth, God has revealed to one of his prophets the entire course of Osmo's life, which the prophet had dutifully recorded and published. Though ignored for many years, it is finally found by Osmo, to whom it brings great discomfort, for it describes with complete accuracy his past and present situations. It also describes his future including how he will die. Taylor concludes that Osmo can justifiably believe that fatalism is true, that the events described in the book are simply unavoidable. Taylor then asks whether fatalism is correct, which amounts to asking whether our situation is significantly different from Osmo's. Concerning this question, Taylor says:

> The important thing to note is that, of the two considerations that explain Osmo's fatalism, only one of them was philosophically relevant, and that one applies to us no less than to him. The two considerations were: (1) there existed a true set of statements about his life, both past and future, and (2) he came to know what those statements were and to believe them. Now the second of these two considerations explains why, as a matter of psychological fact, Osmo became fatalistic, but it has nothing to do with the validity of that point of view. Its validity is assured by (1) alone.
>
> Each of us has but one possible past, described by that totality of statements about us in the past tense, each of which happens to be true. No one ever thinks of rearranging things there; it is simply accepted as given. But so also, each of us has but one possible future, described by that totality of statements about oneself in the future

tense, each of which happens to be true. The sum of these constitutes one's biography.[18]

Taylor claims that there is nothing special about God's foreknowledge upon which fatalistic arguments hinge, for the argument is as easily formulable without reference to God or any other being's knowledge. It is sufficient for the purposes of the argument that certain propositions about the future are true. So it is the mere fact that there are true statements about the future that is sufficient to show that the future is unavoidable; the reference to God, to belief, to written form drops out.

Some clarity about the form of this argument will help us to see how it fails. As I understand it, Taylor's argument goes:

(1) There is a set of propositions about the future which are (now) true.
(2) If there is a set of true propositions about the future, then the future is unavoidable.
(3) If the future is unavoidable, then no action is a free action.
(4) Therefore, no action is a free action.

The passages above taken from Boethius might be interpreted as a close cousin of this argument. In place of (1), he might be claiming that God knows every proposition that will be true. In place of (2), we would have that what God knows must necessarily come about; and then in place of (3), we get the claim that if the future actions of humans must necessarily come about, then those actions are not free, from which (4) follows. Thus, though there is a difference of wording between Taylor's argument for ordinary fatalism and this interpretation of Boethius' arguments, what those arguments rest on are quite similar.

The critical premise in this argument, as I see it, is (2), and it is ambiguous. To say that the future is unavoidable if there is a set of true propositions about it is to make a modal claim. Let us consider two times t and t' such that t' is later than t, and let us consider a set of propositions $p_1 \ldots p_n$, such that member (i) of that set is of the form 'state of affairs A_i occurs at t''. Premise (1) tells us that each member of that set is true at t (the present moment). Given these parameters, (2) can be read either as claiming:

(2') It is a necessary truth that if $p_1 \ldots p_n$ are all true at t, then it will be true at t' that $A_1 \ldots A_n$ obtain.

or

(2″)   If $p_1 \ldots p_n$ are all true at t, then it is necessarily true that it will be true at t' that $A_1 \ldots A_n$ obtain.

(2″) claims that there is only one possible future on the assumption that propositions about the future are true or false (now). If (2″) is true, I think the argument is unassailable. Yet what reason is there to think that (2″) is true? None as far as I can see; further, there is plenty of reason to think it is false. It is intuitively obvious, as I defended in Chapter 1, that there are true claims about the future; it is also intuitively obvious that there is more than one possible world even if there are true claims about the future. Indeed, this is just what (2″) denies. Contrary to the obvious truth that Nixon might have won the election in 1960, (2″) denies this possibility. Here (2″) is obviously wrong; no contradiction is implied by the proposition *Nixon wins the presidential race of 1960*. That claim is false, but it is not contradictory. Thus, in addition to having no good reason for accepting (2″), there is overwhelming reason to reject it.

On the other hand, if the argument employs (2′) rather than (2″), it will have a different false premise. In order for the antecedent of (3) to match the consequent of (2), we will have to distribute the necessity operator in (2′) so that it reads: if it is a necessary truth that $p_1 \ldots p_n$ are true at t, then it is a necessary truth that, at t', $A_1 \ldots A_n$ obtain. The argument, with this alteration, is no longer valid unless the first premise is altered to claim that the true propositions about the future are not only true, but are necessarily true. But, of course, this revised first premise is just a statement of the doctrine of fatalism, and we have already seen the implausibility of this doctrine. Hence, if we read premise (2) as (2′), the alterations required in the argument to make it valid result in an argument which assumes the doctrine of fatalism from the very first premise. Since we have good reason to reject that doctrine, we have good reason to reject this argument for the incompatibility thesis, for on either reading of premise (2), the argument is faulty.

The argument for theological fatalism is subject to the same sort of objection. In place of premise (2), the claim is that what God knows must necessarily come about; yet this premise is subject to the same ambiguity of scope which the original premise (2) is: it may mean that it is a necessary truth that if God knows something, it will come about; or it may mean that if God knows something, then what He knows is a necessary truth. Just as with Taylor's argument, there is no reason to accept the second reading; but if we accept the first, we shall have to alter the first premise to affirm fatalism from the start. Thus, in either case, the argument is defective; so, I conclude the argument for the incompabibility thesis based on features of the future fails.

FREEDOM AND THE PAST

There is one other argument for the incompatibility thesis that centres, not on certain features about the future, but rather on certain features about the past. This objection is clearly formulated by Aquinas, though the general concern can be found earlier – in particular, the argument quoted from Boethius in the last section is probably best taken as a version of this argument. In any case, Aquinas' formulation of it is:

> [E]very conditional proposition, of which the antecedent is absolutely necessary, must have an absolutely necessary consequent. For the antecedent is to the consequent as principles are to the conclusion: and from necessary principles only a necessary conclusion can follow ... But this is a true conditional proposition, *If God knew that this thing will be, it will be*, for the knowledge of God is only of true things. Now, the antecedent of this conditioned proposition is absolutely necessary, because it is eternal, and because it is signified as past. Therefore the consequent is also absolutely necessary. Therefore whatever God knows is necessary; and so the knowledge of God is not of contingent things.[19]

Aquinas here speaks of God's knowledge of contingent things rather than of free actions, but since for Aquinas a contingent thing is just something that is not causally determined and since the sort of freedom in question here is anti-deterministic freedom, this objection is equally an objection to the possibility of free actions given Divine foreknowledge.

The argument has as a crucial premise a claim about a certain feature concerning the past; in particular, the past is fixed, it is beyond the power of any agent to alter. In the light of this necessity of the past, the argument concludes that no human action is free because God knew in the past what action would be performed. The logical principle that completes the argument is this: necessarily, if p implies q, then necessarily p implies necessarily q. So if God's knowledge has the necessity distinctive of the past, then so do all the actions which He has known in the past would be done. What is that sort of necessity? It is the necessity which attaches to a true proposition which places it beyond the capacity of any agent to alter; hence, future actions are beyond the capacity of any agent to alter.

Recently, Nelson Pike has offered a similar argument for the incompatibility thesis, based on the essential omniscience of God.[20] Aquinas' version appeals only to God's omniscience, and we shall see later that Aquinas' views on the matter are more accurate than are Pike's; but let us pass over that point for now. Pike considers an example in which God knew eighty years ago that Jones mows his lawn on a particular Saturday afternoon (in the future). In order for Jones to perform that action freely, it must be possible that he refrain from mowing. This latter possibility Pike denies. He claims:

> If at the time of the action, Jones had been able to refrain from mowing his lawn, then (the most obvious conclusion would seem to be) at the time of action, Jones was able to do something which would have brought it about that God held a false belief eighty years earlier . . .[21]

There would seem to be options other than the one Pike lists above, and Pike grants that there are:

> So far as I can see, there are only two other alternatives. First, we might try describing it as the power to do something that would have brought it about that God believed otherwise than He did eighty years ago; or secondly, we might try describing it as the power to do something that would have brought it about that God (who, by hypothesis, existed eighty years earlier) did not exist eighty years earlier.[22]

Certainly the second of these opinions is unacceptable to the theist, but what about the first? Pike says, 'No action performed at a given time can alter the fact that a given person held a certain belief at a time prior to the time in question.'[23] This claim is just a specific instance of the claim that Aquinas used in his version of the argument: that no person has power over the past. Hence, in both Pike and Aquinas, we find another type of argument for the incompatibility thesis; one which employs certain features that the past has in virtue of which God's foreknowledge (or essential foreknowledge) is incompatible with human freedom.

Let us look more carefully at Pike's argument. As I understand it, it runs:

(5) There is a true set of propositions about the future whose members are such that God has always (in the past) believed of them that they are true.

(6) If S's doing A at t' is a free action, then S is able to refrain from doing A at t'.

(7) If S is able to refrain from doing A at t' and God has always in the past believed that S will do A at t', then either (i) S is able to bring it about that God has a false belief at some time t in the past, (ii) S is able to bring it about that God does not exist at t, or (iii) S is able to bring it about that God does not have a belief at t which God had at t.

(8) Options (i) and (ii) of (7) are not possible.

(9) S is able to bring it about that God does not have a belief at t which God had at t only if one is able to change the past.

(10) No one is able to change the past.

(11) Therefore, S's doing A at t' is not done freely.

Further, this conclusion is perfectly general: it applies to every action by every person, and thus the argument, if sound, is a demonstration of the incompatibility thesis. If the argument is sound, then, if God has known what persons will do in the future, what those persons do cannot be freely done.

Plantinga, in *God, Freedom, and Evil*, considers the argument of Pike's and rejects it.[24] In particular, he rejects premise (7). Both (i) and (ii) in the consequent of (7) involve the same consideration; namely, the possibility of a human agent's bringing it about that God has a false belief. For the consideration under which Pike allows that (ii) might follow involves everyone who had a certain belief about what Jones would do on Saturday having a false belief. Then, if one of these individuals was thought to be God, it would follow that he in fact was not since he would not be omniscient. But this possibility rests on the same possibility as does clause (i): namely, the possibility of Jones doing something that brings it about that God (or the person we thought was God) has a false belief.

Now Plantinga claims that neither (i) (and hence not (ii)) nor (iii) follows from the antecedent of (7). With respect to (iii), he claims,

> What about
> (53) It was within Jones' power at T2 to do something that would have brought it about that God did not hold the belief He did hold at T1?

Here the first problem is one of understanding. How are we to take this proposition? One way is this. What (53) says is that it was within Jones' power, at T2, to do something such that if he had done it, then at T1 God would have held a certain belief and also not held that belief. That is, (53) so understood attributes to Jones the power to bring about a contradictory state of affairs (call this interpretation (53a)). (53a) is obviously and resoundingly false; but there is no reason whatever to think that (51) (the antecedent of (7) above) entails it. What (51) entails is rather

> (53b) It was within Jones' power at T2 to do something such that if he had done it, then God would not have held a belief that in fact he did hold.

This follows from (51) but is perfectly innocent.[25]

To see that Plantinga is right that (53b) is perfectly innocent, recall again the standard semantics for counterfactuals that we discussed in the last section of this chapter. To say that if *p* were true, *q* would have been, is to make a claim about certain possible worlds in which *p* is true. The claim is that in those worlds, any world in which *q* is false is farther from the actual world than any world in which *q* is true. (53b) thus asserts that in that possible world closest to our world in which Jones uses the power in question and does not mow his lawn, God does not believe that he mows his lawn; and that clearly does not assert anything paradoxical.

Plantinga's reason for rejecting that Jones can bring it about that God has a false belief, if he is able to refrain from mowing, is similar. He asks:

> Does (51) entail (52)? No. (52) says that it was within Jones' power to do something – namely, refrain from doing X – such that if he had done that thing, then God *would have* held a false belief at T1. But this does not follow from (5). If Jones had refrained from X, then a proposition that God *did in fact* believe would have been false; but if Jones had refrained from X at T2, then God (since He is omniscient) *would not have believed at T1 that Jones will do X at T2* – indeed, He would have held the true belief that Jones will *refrain* from doing X at T2. What follows from (51) is not (52) but only (52'):
>
>> (52') It was within Jones' power to do something such that if he had done it, then a belief that God *did hold* at T1 *would have been* false.
>
> But (52') is not at all paradoxical and in particular does not imply

that it was within Jones' power to do something that would have brought it about that God held a false belief.[26]

Plantinga's response here is much the same as his last response. Jones' power does result in the truth of certain counterfactuals, but Plantinga insists that Pike reads too much of the actual world into those counterfactuals. Pike wishes to include in the world(s) under consideration that God holds the same beliefs as he does in this world; in such a case, Jones would have the power to make God have a false belief or to make God both hold and not hold the same belief at the same time. Plantinga insists that, since God is omniscient, he would not hold the same beliefs in those worlds; hence Jones does have power, but not the power to make God have a false belief or to do something impossible, but rather only the power to make God hold a belief other than the one He actually holds. Thus, according to Plantinga, (7) is false; hence this argument does not show that freedom and foreknowledge are incompatible.

Yet, it would seem, Plantinga has missed the force of the argument which Pike and Aquinas have formulated. For central to their formulations is the claim that the past is fixed in a certain way, and is beyond the power of any agent to affect. Yet Plantinga gives no argument against this claim; his claims merely imply that it is false. He allows that Jones does have power over the past in that Jones can bring it about that something that was in fact true would not have been true; and it might appear that this is just to allow, contrary to what seems obviously true, that there is power over the past.

Pike responds to Plantinga's rejection of his argument in precisely this fashion.[27] He insists that there is no such thing as power over the past, and that no agent can have the power to perform an action which is such that, were he to perform it, the past would have been different. Pike says:

> Plantinga has not formulated the question correctly. He has not taken account of the restrictions that must be respected if one is to employ a possible worlds analysis of what it is for something to be within one's power. The question is not whether there is just some possible world or other in which Jones refrains from doing X at T2. What must be asked is whether there is a possible world, *having a history prior to T2 that is indistinguishable from that of the actual world*, in which Jones refrains from doing X at T2. The answer is that there is not. All such worlds contain an essentially omniscient being

who believes at T1 that Jones does X at T2. There is no possible world of *this* description in which Jones refrains from doing X at T2.[28]

Pike claims that in responding to his argument, Plantinga has not taken seriously enough our lack of power over the past. Plantinga's answer to Pike's argument seems to imply that, in the sorts of circumstances Jones finds himself, Jones had the power to alter the past. Yet Plantinga does not defend that such power is possible. So, Pike's point in the above quote is that Plantinga's response to the argument does not take seriously enough how the alternative possible worlds (where we are to evaluate the truth of the counterfactuals in question) must be like ours.

On the other hand, Pike's construal of what the alternative worlds must be like is surely too strong. He insists that worlds where the truth of counterfactuals are to be evaluated must have a history 'indistinguishable from that of the actual world'. This is impossible. For every truth about the future, there is also a proposition expressed by a claim of the form 'it has always been the case that such-and-such will happen'. If one insists that the history of another world be indistinguishable from the history of our world, it follows that the worlds themselves are indistinguishable; and worlds which are indistinguishable in the sense that they are constituted by all and only the same true propositions are identical.

Now suppose we accept Pike's account of what worlds must be like for a person to have power to do otherwise: he claims that there must be another world whose history is indistinguishable from ours in which the person does otherwise. As just shown, however, no world is both different from ours and yet has an indistinguishable history from ours, hence it is logically impossible that there be such a world in which a person does otherwise. There are two points of note, then, on Pike's account. First, on his account, no person ever has power to do otherwise than he does, and second, the features of his account that generate this conclusion include no reference to God's foreknowledge at all. Fatalism is generated on Pike's account in a purely non-theological manner. So two conclusions follow. The first is that the problem here is not one concerning God's foreknowledge and what it implies, for the conclusion that humans are not free follows from Pikean premises that make no reference to God. Further, we have good reason to reject Pike's specific argument for the same reasons we have already given for rejecting fatalism. Fatalism is the view that claims that there is only one possible world, and that claim is simply and obviously false. Since Pike's statements imply fatalism, we have good reason to reject it.

ACCIDENTAL NECESSITY

Yet, even if Pike's specific argument implies fatalism, it is not clear that the argument which centres on features of the past must imply fatalism. There is still the worry that in some intuitive sense, the past cannot be altered. Perhaps Pike's construal of what is to be counted as part of the unalterable past is too strong; but, even if this is so, it is far from obvious that God's beliefs which He has held at various points in the past are part of the overly strong elements in Pike's construal. Might it not be, and aren't we strongly tempted to think, that if we clarify properly what is part of the unalterable past, that God's beliefs will be a part of the unalterable past?

What we need here is a way of determining what is really and not just apparently about the past. It is fairly easy to see that this issue cannot be settled by considering whether a proposition is about the past or not, for we can take any proposition that p which is intuitively not about the past and construct a proposition which is about the past merely by adding to *p* the phrase 'it has always been that', thereby generating a new proposition *it has always been that p* which is about the past (because of the phrase 'it has always been that'). Yet there is an air of artificiality in taking this new proposition to be really, or strictly, about the past; if *p* by itself is about the present or future, it is natural to say that *it has always been that p* is infected by this presentness or futurity – *it has always been that p* is just not really, or strictly, about the past.

Accidental Necessity *via* Power Over the Past

The reason we are interested in what is strictly about the past is that we are granting that there is a certain sort of necessity that attaches to such claims. Let us, with the medieval logicians, call this sort of necessity 'accidental necessity'. The question then is: under what conditions is a proposition accidentally necessary? My suggestion above might be taken as claiming that a proposition is accidentally necessary if and only if it is strictly about the past.

Our interest here in the past is a sort of intervening variable, for what is really critical about the past is our intuition that it is really beyond our control (in a way in which the future is not). Perhaps, then, we could define accidental necessity simply in terms of what we have control over, and dispense with the intervening notion of what is strictly about the past. In a recent article, Plantinga attempts to do just this.[29] His definition is:

> AN1: p is accidentally necessary at t if and only if (i) p is true at t, and (ii) it is not possible both that (i) and that there exist agents $S_1 \ldots S_n$ and actions $A_1 \ldots A_n$ such that (a) A_i is basic for S_i, (b) each S_i has the power at t or later to perform A_i, and (c) necessarily, if every S_i were to perform A_i at t or later, then p would have been false.[30]

In order to understand AN1, we need a clarification of what it is for an action to be basic for a person. Plantinga claims:

> D1:   Action A is basic for a person S if and only if there is an action A^* that S can directly perform, and which is such that his being in normal conditions and performing A^* is causally sufficient for his performing A.[31]

Though he does not offer a clarification of what it is to perform an action directly, Plantinga does give a sufficient condition for the capacity to perform an action directly. He claims that an action is one that a person can perform directly if it can be performed without having to perform some other action in order to perform it.[32] He cites as an example Chisholm's suggestion that the only actions that can be performed directly are undertakings – undertaking to raise one's arm, for example. Given Plantinga's claims, perhaps he would assent to:

> P1:   Action A is directly performed by S if (i) S does A, and (ii) there is no action A' such that necessarily, S does A only if S does A'.

A note of clarification is in order here about these definitions. If AN1 is to be adequate, any directly performed action must also be a basic action, for otherwise AN1 will imply that all actions to be performed in the future which will be directly performed are now accidentally necessary, i.e. we cannot have the power to do otherwise than perform them. It is not clear that D1 implies that direct performances count as basic actions, for one can take the notion of causal sufficiency to exclude logical sufficiency. Thus, since directly performing A^* is logically sufficient for performing A^*, it might be claimed that D1 excludes A^* from being a basic action. I suggest that we take causal sufficiency not to exclude logical sufficiency to avoid having to alter D1.

Therefore, if directly performing $A*$ is logically sufficient for performing A, I shall assume that D1 implies that A is a basic action.

Though P1 does not completely clarify the notion of direct performance, perhaps it is adequate enough to give us a reasonably clear idea of what Plantinga has in mind in AN1. What AN1 claims, then, is that a proposition is accidentally necessary if and only if it is true and it is not possible that it be true and there be a set of basic actions which, if performed by some set of agents having the power to perform them, would entail that p is false.

To catch a sense of what Plantinga has in mind, let us consider a couple of examples. Consider the proposition that I will get up tomorrow at 5.30 am. Is this proposition accidentally necessary? It ought not to be so, and AN1 implies that it is not. First, suppose it is true; if it is, what we need to know is whether it is possible that it be true and there be a set of basic actions which, if performed, would entail that it is false. And, of course, that is possible: all I need to do is to remain in bed till 5.35; my doing that entails that I do not rise at 5.30.

Consider as another example the proposition that Columbus discovered America. If we assume that this proposition is true, it ought to turn out to be accidentally necessary, and AN1 has this implication. It is not possible that it be true and there be basic actions which, if performed, would entail that it is false. There may be actions that, if performed, would have resulted in the falsity of that proposition; perhaps, for example, God would have prevented anyone from discovering America if some person were to perform a certain action tomorrow (say, for example, if Reagan were to issue some command which would result in nuclear war tomorrow, God, in order to prevent the war, would not have allowed Columbus to discover America). We might describe an action like this that has implications for the past as an action requiring the fore-co-operation of God. It is not that the action requires the possibility of backward causation; rather, the difference such an action would have made in the past requires God's fore-co-operation. But, even if there are such actions which (given God's fore-co-operation) would have resulted in Columbus' not having discovered America, the performance of that action would not *entail* the falsity of the proposition that Columbus discovered America (for example, He could have prevented Reagan from performing the actions necessary to start a war by causing him to be paralysed). Hence that proposition is accidentally necessary.

There is a technical problem with AN1, though. It arises from the fact that counterfactuals with necessarily false antecedents, on the standard semantics which Plantinga accepts, are necessarily true. Consider the following case. The agents in question are God and Ronald Reagan, and the respective actions are *preventing Ronald Reagan from eating Cheerios tomorrow* and *eating Cheerios tomorrow*. Presumably, God has the power to perform the first action and Ronald Reagan the second; further, if such actions were performed they would be basic actions. However, it is impossible that both God and Reagan both perform their respective actions; hence the antecedent of (c) of AN1 is necessarily false regarding this set of agents and actions. Given that the antecedent is necessarily false, clause (c) is vacuously true, *regardless of what proposition the proposition that p happens to be.* Hence, for any true proposition, the God–Reagan case above shows that clauses (i)–(iii) of AN1 are satisfied for any such proposition. For any true proposition *p*, AN1 implies that *p* is accidentally necessary.

This defect is not difficult to remedy, though; we merely need to add the restriction that the conjunctive performance of all the acts in question is possible. We then get:

AN2:   *p* is accidentally necessary at *t* if and only if (i) *p* is true at *t* and (ii) it is not possible both that (i) and that there exist agents $S_1 \ldots S_n$ and actions $A_1 \ldots A_n$ such that (a) A_i is basic for S_i, (b) each S_i has the power at *t* or later to perform A_i, (c) it is possible that every S_i perform A_i at *t* or later, and (d) necessarily, if every S_i were to perform A_i at *t* or later, then *p* would have been false.

AN2 avoids the above problem with AN1 because of its inclusion of the restriction that the performance of all the basic actions in question at *t* or later must be possible. Further, it shares with AN1 the characteristic of defining accidental necessity in terms of the power that agents have.

Assuming for the moment that AN2 is adequate, what implications does it have for the argument for incompatibilism based on the necessity of the past? The first point to note here is that it does not clearly imply that the incompatibilism argument is unsound. The reason it does not is that it is not especially clear what we have power over and what we do not. Plantinga would claim that, on AN2, what God believed yesterday is not accidentally necessary, for if Jones were to act differently today than he actually does, that would entail that God believed something different yesterday (since God is essentially omniscient). Pike, on the other hand, might insist that since what a person believed yesterday is accidentally necessary, Jones does not have the power to act otherwise than he actually does (because God's beliefs can't be wrong). In the absence of a clear account of what we have power over and what we do not, it is not clear that AN2 implies that the incompatibility argument under consideration is unsound.

Yet, if AN2 is adequate, it does undermine the argument in question, for it shows that one of its premises lacks sufficient grounds for acceptance. There are two premises in question here: the first is the claim that if a person brings it about that God has a different belief than He in fact had in the past, then that person has changed the past; the second is the claim that no one can change the past. The sense in which the second is true is when the notion of the past is interpreted as that part of the past that is accidentally necessary. Under this interpretation, though, it is no longer clear (if AN2 is acceptable) that a person must change the past in order to bring it about that God holds a different belief than He in fact held. In order for this claim to be clearly true, it must be shown that no one has the power to do something which is necessarily such that, if done, God's beliefs would have been different. Perhaps such an argument can be constructed (though I do not see how); in any case, no such argument has been constructed, and until one is given, there is no good reason to accept the premise in question. Thus, were AN2 acceptable, the incompatibility argument would be undermined.

However, AN2 is not acceptable, and we can see by considering a purported counter-example to it. This example concerns the nature of God's actions; in particular, it concerns the fact that most of God's actions are basic actions. Now, clearly, there are some of God's actions which are not basic – for example, his acting so as to improve my moral character. It is not clear that D1 implies that this action is not basic, for it is not positive whether the 'normal conditions' clause excludes my co-operating with God. Yet some of Plantinga's examples seem to indicate that the clause should not include such co-operation among agents; for instance, he claims that his starting a war is not a basic action. If it is not, I would think this is so partly because the 'normal conditions' clause is meant to exclude the co-operation of reactions of other agents to what a person does. And just so with God's action of improving my moral character. Nothing God can do can entail that my moral character is improved apart from my co-operation. So when God's actions are directed at states of affairs that require the co-operation of other free agents, his actions are not basic actions.

None the less, it is still true that many of God's actions are basic. For example, any of his acts such as conserving nature, affecting the natural order, performing miracles, etc., will be basic actions. In these domains, there is no co-operation required in order for God to accomplish his purposes, hence these actions are basic. In fact, an even stronger claim can be made here; most of God's actions on the natural order of things are actions which he performs directly. This fact is reflected by Plantinga's understanding of direct performance in P1. In particular, what God does, does not require his performing some other action in order to be performed. So when God performs a miracle, or sustains the universe, he performs such actions directly.

The counter-example arises from consideration of the following proposition:

(12) God has the power to perform an action A such that if He were to do A at t without at some earlier time having brought it about that some event did not occur which is now a matter of history, God would have done a moral wrong.

On intuitive grounds, what (12) claims is that there are things God could do which are such that if He did them in a world with the same history as ours, His performing that action would result in his having committed a moral wrong. (12) is at least possibly true; examples of the sort required can be constructed by imagining God promising to do something that on all other grounds, other than the fact that He promised to do it, is morally neutral. Since the act itself is morally neutral and is not logically impossible, even a perfectly good God could perform it. What a perfectly good God could not do, however, is fail to perform it once He has promised to do it, for the act of promising turns an otherwise neutral act into a required act. So the neutral acts are ones that God can perform; further, if He in the past promised to perform those acts, then the act in question is one such that if He performed it without having done something different in the past, He would have committed a moral wrong. Hence (12) is possibly true.

Consider, then, a world in which (12) is true, and let p be a conjunctive proposition giving the entire history of the world, including the fact that God has made a promise of the sort described in (12); it would seem that p should then turn out to be accidentally necessary. What I wish to argue is that, on the assumption that (12) is true, p is not accidentally necessary on AN2 (and hence not on AN1 either).

The first requirement of AN2 is automatically satisfied, so I shall concentrate on the second. Let the set of agents in question have only one member, God; and let the set of actions in question be A in (12) above, an action which is a basic action for God (i.e. one that requires no human co-operation, or the co-operation of any other free agents).

It then follows that clauses (a), (b), and (c) of (ii) are satisfied. If we can also show that clause (d) is satisfied, we will have shown that proposition *p* is not accidentally necessary on AN2, and thus that AN2 is inadequate. The argument that (d) is true makes critical use of

(13) it is not possible that God can commit a moral wrong,

which follows from God's essential moral goodness.

By (13), then, the consequent of (12) is impossible; thus in order for (12) to be true, its antecedent must be impossible as well. Hence we get:

(14) it is not possible that God both does *A* and does not make *p* false.

Since we have already granted that God has the power to do actions of the sort described in (12), it follows that if He were to do *A*, He would have to make *p* false. Thus, clause (d) is satisfied; it is necessarily true that if God were to do *A*, *p* would have been false. Hence, AN2 implies that the proposition which would seem to be just a strict history of the past is not accidentally necessary.

There is, however, a response left open to a defender of AN2, and it is to suggest that God in fact does not have the power at the time in question to perform the act in question, nor need He have that power in order to be omnipotent. The reason for this is that, in clarifying the claim that a being is omnipotent, we should say that a being is omnipotent only if that being can bring about any state of affairs at *t* in a world that someone in a world with the same history as that world can bring about at *t*.[33] The reason for this is that it is just as clearly a mistake to require an omnipotent being to be able to "undo" what is accidentally necessary as it is to require that an omnipotent being be able to do things that cannot be done in general. If this point is granted, one might allow that what God promised to do in the past is accidentally necessary. Allowing this, though, prohibits us from holding that God has the power to do the action described in (12), for there is no possible world *with the same history as the one in question* in which anyone performs that action; hence, not even an omnipotent being could do it.

I am not convinced that this response is adequate, for in order for it to absolve AN2, the following principles must be true: if in a set of circumstances, to do A is to do B, and it is not possible to do B, then it is not possible to do A. In the counter-example above, B is the breaking of a promise and A is the act which God promised to do. The principle, though, seems clearly false; all that follows is that it is not possible to do A *in the circumstances in question*. But that act is not the same as the act of doing A.

Even if the principle is true, though, the counter-example above shows that we cannot define accidental necessity as in AN2. For the response to the counter-example shows that in order to define the notion of power appealed to in AN2, we will have to appeal to the notion of accidental necessity itself. In particular, we shall have to define God's power in terms of what can be done in a world with the same history as this one.

My point here, then, is as follows. We began thinking that we needed an account of what was strictly about the past in order to settle the dispute between Plantinga and Pike; but we were deterred in undertaking this task by the suggestion that we could simply define the notion of accidental necessity in question by the notion of the power that agents have. We now see that proceeding in this direction was only a detour, for in order to employ AN2, we need a clarification of what individuals have power over; and to do that, we shall have to clarify what is strictly about the past. Hence, even if AN2 could avoid the counter-example above, it would not be an adequate definition of accidental necessity; for the notion of power it employs must itself be defined in terms of what is accidentally necessary. We must return, therefore, to the task of clarifying what is strictly about the past.

Accidental Necessity *Via* the Distinction Between Hard and Soft Facts

The fundamental intuition at work concerning what the past is strictly about is a claim whose truth-value depends solely on some particular moment, or series of moments, in the past. Thus, for example, when we prefix a claim about the future with a past tense operator, we do not end up with a proposition strictly about the past, for the proposition in question does not pick out any event which occurred wholly at some moment which used to be a present moment; there is no time in the past when the truth of the proposition in question results from what was purely present at that time. When a proposition is strictly about the past, I shall say that what it expresses is a hard fact about the past, reflecting the insight that what is strictly about the past is fixed. If a proposition is not strictly about the past, but is still about the past in some sense, I shall refer to what it expresses as a soft fact about the past, reflecting the insight that such facts need not be beyond the power of any agent to affect. Recently Marilyn Adams has suggested an account of the distinction between hard and soft facts. We are assuming that:

AN3: p is accidentally necessary at $t =_{df.} p$ is strictly about the past, i.e. the fact which p expresses is a hard fact.

Adams claims:

D2: Proposition p expresses a hard fact about time $t =_{df.} p$ is not at least in part about any time t' such that t' is later than t .[34]

And she clarifies the notion of being in part about a time as:

D3: Proposition p is at least in part about $t =_{df.}$ the happening or not happening, the actuality or non-actuality, of something at t is a necessary condition for p 's being true.[35]

The intuition behind Adams' account is the intuition discussed above: a hard fact about a time is a fact whose obtaining at that time is independent of what happens at any later time than the time in question. As Adams puts it, the proposition in question is not even in part about any time later than the time in question.

This account, though, is inadequate. Its inadequacy arises from considering the various possibilities for clarifying the crucial notion of a necessary condition in D3.[36] There are three options that I can think of, corresponding to the three types of implication: material implication, counterfactual implication, and strict implication. Clearly, we cannot use the notion of material implication to interpret the notion of a necessary condition, for every truth is a materially necessary condition for every other truth. Hence on the material implication understanding, no proposition would express a hard fact.

The notion of strict implication alleviates this difficulty, but it has problems of its own. First, there are soft facts expressed by relations between future truths and past events; for example, consider the soft fact that Reagan's election preceded my completing this book by six years. Since I have not yet completed this book, and since Reagan was elected in 1980, it is within my power to alter the truth of that proposition. Yet does it strictly imply any proposition about a time later than the present? No, it does not; it only does so on the assumptions that Reagan was elected in 1980 and that it is not yet 1986.

Or, consider a different sort of problem for D3 on this interpretation. Fischer gives as an example the proposition *either Smith knew at t that Jones would do X at t' or Jones believed at t that Jones would do X at t'*, where t' is later than t .[37] This proposition should not express a hard fact at any moment between t and t', unless Jones had the belief in question at t. So suppose Jones does not have that belief at t; then that proposition should express a soft fact since it is within Jones' power to make the entire disjunction false. Yet, on D3, that proposition expresses a hard fact, for it does not entail that anything happens after t. The first disjunct by itself does, but the entire disjunction does not. Hence D3 improperly implies that this proposition expresses a hard fact.

Fischer mentions one other problem. He correctly claims that the proposition *Smith existed yesterday* should, if true, express a hard fact.[38] Yet this proposition does not express a hard fact on the interpretation of D3 we are considering, for it entails that it is not the case that Smith will exist for the first time tomorrow. And so more generally: any claim of the sort that X existed at t will entail that it is false that X existed for the first time at t' (later than t). We thus have another reason for rejecting the strict implication interpretation of D3.

So neither the material implication nor strict implication interpretation of Adams' phrase 'necessary condition' is trouble free. The last interpretation is the counterfactual conditional. Examination of this interpretation is simple, for though it may avoid some of the problems with the other interpretations above, it at least shares the last problem with the strict implication interpretation. Since an entailment relation holds between the propositions that Smith existed yesterday and that it is false that Smith will exist for the first time tomorrow, a counterfactual implication holds between these propositions as well. Therefore, the counterfactual interpretation is not free from difficulty either.

Perhaps some reflection on what the distinction between hard and soft facts is supposed to be will help us here.[39] First, a hard fact is a fact about the past; this point commits us to the two following necessary conditions for hard facts:

(N1) p expresses a hard fact at time t only if p is true,

and

(N2) p expresses a hard fact at time t only if the moment immediately preceding t is a past time.

Another point to note about hard facts is that there is a certain time at which they "hardened". Soft facts are facts which have not, so to speak, become hard yet. This point implies:

(N3) p expresses a hard fact at time t only if p is not a necessary truth.

The notion of "hardening" has another implication. This implication is that accidental necessity is, generally, something a proposition comes to have at a certain time. So the acquisition of hardness is generally locatable at a specific point (or duration) of time.

To express this point properly is somewhat complicated, but perhaps we can make some headway as follows. What we want to do is to pick out the point in time at which the fact which a proposition expresses becomes fixed. How can we do this? I suggest we pick out the moment in question by considering at what point the proposition in question could have been expressed by a present-tense sentence. So the point at which the proposition *Lincoln freed the slaves in 1864* expresses a fact which has just become a hard fact is the moment immediately following the moment at which an utterance of 'Lincoln is (now) freeing the slaves', where the word 'now' picks out the year 1864, would have expressed that proposition.

There is one complication concerning this point. If we were sure that there was a first moment of time, we could capture this notion of "hardening" as described above. However, suppose there is no first moment of time, and suppose God has, from all eternity, been creating some physical universe or other.[40] Then the proposition *there has always been a physical universe* should turn out to be accidentally necessary, yet there will be no point at which that truth can be expressed by a present-tense sentence. Let us call such propositions as this 'immemorial propositions'. An immemorial proposition is one that is true and is such that its truth cannot, at any time, be expressed without employing some past tense sentence. Our point about "hardening" then requires the following disjunctive condition:

(N4) p expresses a hard fact at time t only if either (i) for some time t' earlier than t there is a purely present tense sentence E with meaning M which is such that (a) an utterance of 'E at t'', where E has meaning M, would express the truth that p, and (b) an utterance of 'E at t'', where E has meaning M and where the referential force of E is the same as t', would not express p; or (ii) p is an immemorial proposition.

There are two as yet undefined technical notions contained in (N4). To see why we need the notion of a purely present tense sentence, let us consider an example which will also help us get a clearer understanding of what (N4) claims. Suppose p is the proposition that Kennedy was President in 1961. In order for this proposition to express a hard fact about times after 1961, the sentence 'Kennedy is President in 1961' has to express p at some time prior to times later than 1961. What time is that? The time is 1961, of course. Further, that same sentence has to fail to express a truth at any time later than 1961. Does it? On the face of it, it is not clear, for the sentence in question is ambiguous between a sentence where the word 'is' means 'is now' and a sentence where the word 'is' means 'is tenselessly'. The second sentence does express a truth at a later time than 1961, and also expresses a truth if uttered at any time before 1961. However, the first sentence ('Kennedy is now President in 1961') only expresses a true proposition if the temporal index is the time referred to by the temporal indexical 'now'. Hence this sentence only expresses a true proposition if uttered in 1961. So if we take the sentence in question to be the one whose verb means 'is now', then at any time other than 1961 the sentence in question could not express a true proposition.

I have included the requirement that the present tense sentence referred to in (N4) is a *purely* present tense sentence to handle this ambiguity between a tenseless 'is' and a tensed 'is'. We can define that notion as follows:

PPTS: *E*, having meaning *M*, is a purely present tense sentence if and only if (i) *E* is a present tense sentence whose verb '——' or '———s' means '——— now' or '———s now.'

There is also another technical expression contained in (N4), having to do with the constancy of the referential force of a sentence expressed at two different times. In order to appreciate the need for such a restriction, suppose the sentence which expresses a truth at t is a sentence containing indexicals or demonstratives such as 'I', 'he', 'it', 'this', 'that', etc. In some views, the meaning of such words remains constant when used on different occasions to pick out different objects, times, etc.; in other views, the meaning of such terms is systematically ambiguous because the reference is different on different occasions of use. We need not determine which of these views is correct, for we can accommodate either view. If meaning is determined by reference, the above conditions are adequate as they stand; the only problem is if the meaning is the same even though the reference is different. To see the problem this view raises, consider my expressing the truth that I went home at 3.00 yesterday, by asserting (yesterday) 'I am now going home at 3.00 pm.' When temporally indexed to yesterday's date, the sentence would express a truth if uttered by me; but it might express a falsehood if uttered by someone else. Hence clause (i) of (N4) is false as it stands if the sentence uttered by both me and someone else has the same meaning.

These conditions require the following definition of constancy of referential force:

CRF: An utterance of '*E* at *t*' has the same referential force as an utterance of '*E* at *t'* ' if and only if the reference of any term including indexicals and demonstratives (other than the demonstrative 'now' which is essential to the purely present-tenseness of the sentence) is the same.

The conditions cited so far appear most likely to add up to a conjunctive sufficient condition for something's being a hard fact when the propositions in question are taken to be simple propositions. Complex propositions, such as disjunctions, conjunctions, conditionals, etc., can be misclassified if we take (N1)–(N4) to be jointly sufficient for a proposition to be a hard fact. For example, the above conditions do not properly deal with such sentences as 'Jack knows now that it will rain tomorrow'. This sentence satisfies the requirements of (N4), and yet what it expresses does not have a truth-value independent of all times other than now. We need to add a condition then to deal with complex propositions.

Let A be the set of atomic propositions such that each member of A passes the tests for expressing a hard fact at *t* included in (N4), and let V(A) be the assignment of truth-values to the members of A. We might then attempt to define what it is for a proposition to be independent of certain other times as:

D4: *p* is independent of times later than or including $t =_{\text{df.}}$ (i) if *p* is true, then it is not possible that *p* is false given V(A), and (ii) if *p* is false, then it is not possible that *p* is true given V(A).

This definition, though, will not do, for it addresses the problem of complex propositions only when the complex in question is an *extensional* complex, i.e. one whose form is such that the truth-value of propositions of that form is truth-functional (I am assuming here a propositional, rather than a predicate, logic). However, if the complex in question is *intensional*, D4 is inadequate, for such propositions will not have a truth-value determined by the atomic propositions countenanced in D4. Hence we need an additional clause to deal with such intensional complexes.

We might wish to count any intensional complex which satisfies (N4) as independent in the required sense; however, this would be a mistake.

For the proposition *Reagan knew yesterday that he would fire his staff tomorrow* would then, if true, express a proposition independent of any time after today. Yet its truth-value is clearly dependent on what happens tomorrow.

What we need to do here is to distinguish pure from impure intensional complexes. The intuitive idea is that a pure intensional complex is one in which the truth-value of the entire complex does not depend on any of its propositional components for its truth-value. An impure intensional complex is one in which the entire complex does depend on some propositional component being true. We might try to capture this point by altering D4 to:

> D4′: p is independent of times t and after $=_{df.}$ (i) if p is an extensional proposition or complex, then (a) if p is true, then it is not possible that p is false given V(A), and (b) if p is false, then it is not possible that p is true given V(A); and (ii) if p is an intensional complex, then (a) if p is pure, then p passes requirements (N1)–(N4) for expressing a hard fact, and (b) if p is impure, then any component of p which must be true if p is, is independent of times t and after.

Among the intensional complexes referred to in D4′, the primary examples are psychological attitudes. A pure psychological attitude is one that can obtain regardless of whether the object of that attitude is true or not. Thus, believing, hoping, wishing, and wanting are normally pure psychological attitudes; knowing is not. Since such pure attitudes are independent of the truth-value of their component propositions, it is necessary either to count them as atomic or to include a special provision for handling them. Since, intuitively, they are not atomic (because they are composed out of a proposition and an operator), I have chosen to take the latter alternative.

A word is in order here about the notion of an atomic proposition being appealed to. First, a proposition is not atomic if its constituents include separable propositions. So, for example, conjunctions, disjunctions, conditionals, and negations are not atomic propositions; neither are propositions involving propositional attitudes. Thus, if a proposition including a propositional attitude is to be independent of certain times by D4′, the particular propositional attitude must be independent of the truth or falsity of its object or the object of the attitude must itself be independent of those times. Hence propositions such as *David knows that p* will be independent of certain times only if p is independent of those times, whereas propositions such as *Reagan believes the Russians will remain evil* is independent of certain times even though the object of the attitude is not.

Second, it is obvious that the distinction between atomic and complex cannot be made perfectly clear without an appeal to the notion of a proper philosophical analysis of a proposition. If the best analysis of a proposition analyses it into component propositions, then the proposition is not atomic. Though this requirement is not perfectly clear, I do not think the lack of clarity will affect the way in which the distinction is employed in evaluating the argument for the incompatibility between foreknowledge and freedom.

Assuming the acceptability of D4' (which we will come to question), we could affirm:

D5: p expresses a hard fact at $t =_{df.}$ (i) p is independent of times later than or including t, and (ii) p passes requirements (N1)–(N3).

Further, D5 allows us to define the notion of a hard fact:

D6: p expresses a hard fact $=_{df.}$ there is some time prior to or including the present moment at which p expresses a hard fact.

The conjunction of D5, D6, and AN3 is an account of accidental necessity which preserves the intuition that what is most truly real is what is presently occurring, independently of what has taken place in the past or what will take place in the future. The past is only what used to be present, the future only what will be; the present is ontologically fundamental. Hence there ought to be a distinction between claims about any particular time which describe ontologically fundamental features of that moment, and claims about a particular time which do not describe such features. My suggestion has been that the sort of claim which describes an ontologically fundamental feature is one expressible by the use of a purely present tense sentence at some point. It is the propositions expressed by such sentences in addition to immemorial propositions which are fundamental in understanding what a hard fact is. Finally, it is the class of hard facts which delimits the class of accidentally necessary truths.

Consideration of a few examples will help in understanding how the above definitions work. So let us see how this account fares against Fischer's counter-examples to Adams' account.

First, consider the proposition that Reagan's (first) election preceded the completion of this book by five years. Intuitively, that proposition should not turn out to be accidentally necessary, and by our definition it does not. The reason it does not is that this proposition is a complex one, expressible at Reagan's election by the sentences 'Reagan is (now) being elected', and 'It is now five years prior to the completion of this book'. The proposition expressed by this latter sentence, though, is complex as well; it is a conjunction of the claim that it is now a certain date and the claim that in five years a certain book will be completed. Since this last claim is such that it cannot be truly expressed by a present tense sentence five years ago, it is not independent of all times other than the time of Reagan's election; hence it follows that the original proposition is not accidentally necessary.

Consider then the claim that either Smith knew at t that Jones would do X at t' or Jones believed at t that Jones would do X at t', where t' is later than t. This counter-example presupposes that Jones does not have the belief in question, therefore the proposition is true by virtue of what Smith knew at t. One of the implications of D4' is that any disjunction or conjunction is independent of certain times if and only if all its component parts are; hence, since Smith's knowing what Jones would do is not independent of all times later than or including t, the disjunction above is not independent of all times later than or including t. So, by D6, the proposition above does not express a hard fact, and hence is not accidentally necessary.

Finally consider any proposition of the form *S existed at t*. The difficulty for Adam's account is that any proposition of this form entails numerous other propositions of the form *It is not the case that S existed for the first time at t + n*. Propositions having this latter form are not relevant, in my account, to the former since the latter sort are complex propositions which include as a part the proposition that S existed for the first time at $t + n$. This proposition cannot be expressed by a present tense sentence, though, until the time in question arrives; thus the fact that a proposition such as *S existed at t* entails this sort of proposition is irrelevant in my view.

In spite of the success of these definitions in dealing with the cases above, there is a problem with this account in that it has a compatibilist implication since, given it, God's beliefs about what will occur are not strictly about the past. However, the account also implies that God's promises, if the content of the promise is about the future, are not strictly about the past. Given God's nature, if He promises to do something, that entails He will do it; hence any proposition of the form *God has promised to bring it about that p* will be an impure intensional complex. If p itself is about a future time, then it will not be independent of future times; and the proposition about God's promise will not express a hard fact.

Yet, regardless of what we should say about God's beliefs, God's promises should not be soft facts about the past. If we are compatibilists, we shall want to say that God holds a particular belief about the future because that is the way things will turn out. But regarding God's promises, we should say that the order of explanation is reversed: if God promises to bring it about that p, then p's truth is to be explained by the fact that God promised to bring it about.

So we shall have to alter D4′ to:

D4″: p is independent of times t and after $=_{df.}$ (i) if p is an extensional proposition or complex, then (a) if p is true, then it is not possible that p is false given V(A), and (b) if p is false, then it is not possible that p is true given V(A); and (ii) if p is an intensional complex, then (a) if p is pure, then p passes requirements (N1)–(N4) for expressing a hard fact, and (b) if p is impure, then, for any q such that it is not possible that p is true unless q is, then either (i) if the truth of q explains the truth of p, then q is independent of times t and after, or (ii) if the truth of q is explained by the truth of p, then p passes requirements (N1)–(N4).

This definition is recursive. Thus, though the notion being defined is appealed to in the defining, the definition is not circular.

I propose, then, that the account given above is an adequate one concerning accidental necessity. On it, a certain symmetry holds between human and divine foreknowledge, for both propositions of the form *God knew that S will do A* and of the form *Some human S′ knew that S will do A* turn out to express soft facts about the past, and are not accidentally necessary.

The question we must ask, however, concerns the implications of this account for God's beliefs. The critical consideration here is whether God's beliefs explain the truth of what He believes or not. The incompatibilist maintains that the explanatory schema proceeds from beliefs to content, the compatibilist, from content to belief (we must remember here that, in either case, the explanatory relation need not be a causal relation). Therefore, according to the compatibilist, an important asymmetry holds between human cognisers and the Divine cogniser, because propositions of the form *God believed that S will do A* express soft facts about the past, whereas propositions of the form *Some human S′ believed that S will do A* express hard facts about the past. Though the account of accidental necessity presented here does not imply that the compatibility is right, the account, if acceptable, undermines the argument we are considering for incompatibilism. For the incompatibilist argument requires that God's beliefs be hard facts about the past, and given this account of accidental necessity, one has reason to accept this premise only if one has reason to think that the explanatory schema proceeds from God's beliefs to the contents of what He believes. Without such an argument, we can conclude that the incompatibility argument fails.

An even stronger conclusion might follow if an adequate description of what it is for one thing to explain another were available. Such an account might perhaps decide whether belief can explain truth or vice versa. However, in the absence of one, we cannot conclude from this discussion that compatibilism is correct (even if we have good reason to accept the account of accidental necessity above). We do not need such a strong conclusion here, for the goal of this chapter is only to show that there is no good argument for incompatibilism; and that goal can be accomplished if the above account of accidental necessity is defensible and there is no other good argument that God's beliefs must be hard facts. For if it is defensible and no other argument is available, one of the premises in this last argument for incompatibilism is unsupported. So even though it would be nice to have an account of the nature of explanation, the lack of such an account is not damaging. It would be if this chapter were intended to defend compatibilism, but that defence will not be undertaken until the next chapter.

Ontological Basicality and the Incompatibility Thesis

There is a different sort of argument that is intended to show that God's beliefs must be hard facts about the past, regardless of what account of accidental necessity is adequate. The argument claims to provide a constraint which any proposed account of accidental necessity must satisfy. Fischer says:

> Consider the fact that Caesar died 2009 years prior to Saunders' writing his paper. What lies behind our view that this fact is not a hard fact about 44 B.C.? We might say that it is a soft fact about 44 B.C. because *one and the same* physical process would have counted as Caesar's dying 2009 years prior to Saunders' writing his paper, if Saunders wrote his paper in 1965, and would *not* have counted as

Caesar's dying 2009 years prior to Saunders' writing his paper, if Saunders hadn't written his paper in 1965. This captures the "future dependence" of soft facts; a soft fact is a fact in virtue of events which occur in the future.

Similarly, suppose that Smith knew at T1 that Jones would do X at T2. Smith's knowledge is a soft fact about T1 because *one and the same* state of Smith's mind (at T1) would count as knowledge if Jones did X at T2, and would not count as knowledge if Jones didn't do X at T2. Exactly the same sort of future dependence explains why both facts – the fact about Caesar's death and the fact about Smith's knowledge – are soft facts [emphasis mine].[41]

Fischer then goes on to draw the implications of this emphasis on identity of states, processes, etc.:

Thus, an incompatibilist might insist on the following sort of constraint on an account of the hard fact/soft fact distinction: the only way in which God's belief at T1 about Jones at T2 could be a soft fact about the past relative to T2 would be if *one and the same* state of the mind of the person who was God at T1 would count as one belief if Jones did X at T2, but a different belief (or not a belief at all) if Jones did not do X at T2. But it is implausible to suppose that one and the same state of the mind of the person who was God at T1 would count as different beliefs given different behavior by Jones at T2 [emphasis mine].[42]

According to Fischer, for anything to be a soft fact, there must be some other fact which is not a soft fact which comes to have different sorts of characteristics depending on how the future turns out. Thus, in the Caesar case, it is the physical process in question which is not a soft fact; the characteristics which that process acquires depends on whether Saunders writes his paper in 1965 or not. None the less, the physical process itself is the same process regardless of how the future turns out.

Or, again, when humans have foreknowledge, the foreknowledge is a soft fact. This fact is soft by virtue of there being some other fact which is not soft on which the soft fact is ontologically parasitic; in this case it is the state of mind of the person in question. In order for Smith's foreknowledge to be a soft fact, there must be another fact which remains the same, which is knowledge if Jones does one thing and is not knowledge if Jones does another. Smith's state of belief is just this sort of fact.

We then turn to the case of God's foreknowledge and ask: if God's foreknowledge is a soft fact, what hard fact about God is there in virtue of which His foreknowledge is a soft fact? Fischer's requirement implies that there must be some other fact on which this fact depends if this fact is to be a soft fact. If the compatibilist is not able to come up with some such fact on which the soft fact is 'parasitic', the conclusion Fischer thinks should be drawn is that what was thought to be a soft fact is not a soft fact after all. Thus Fischer's argument issues a strong challenge to compatibilists: what is the fact on which God's foreknowledge depends?

The first thing to note is that we cannot say, as in the case of human foreknowledge, that the fact is the belief in question – at least, we cannot say this if we wish to remain compatibilists. For the critical characteristic of the account of accidental necessity presented here – critical for defending compatibilism – is that God's beliefs as well as his knowledge are soft facts. Hence the sort of explanation appropriate in the case of human foreknowledge is not appropriate, if compatibilist conclusions can be defended, in discussing God's foreknowledge. Appealing to God's beliefs is to appeal to another soft fact and it too needs to be parasitic on some other fact (assuming Fischer's criterion is correct).

An answer is not hard to find: God's foreknowledge depends on the fact of His believing the truth. So the compatibilist can find a fact which satisfies Fischer's requirement. He claims that if God's foreknowledge is to be a soft fact, then there must be another on which this soft fact is parasitic and which has one characteristic if one free action is done and another characteristic if a different free action is done. The fact that God believes the truth is just such a fact; if I were to leave early today, that fact would have the characteristic of the truth that I leave early today as the truth in question, and if I choose not to leave early, that fact has a different truth as the one which God believes.

Fischer might complain here that God's believing the truth is not a fact which is ontologically basic enough. He might claim that there are two different states here; one is the state of believing, and the other is the state of believing the truth. He might say that the first is ontologically more basic than the second since it is a proper conceptual part of the second. Then he might insist that – in finding a fact which satisfies his above criterion – no fact can be appealed to for which there is some other soft fact ontologically more basic. Hence, in clarifying the fact that God's foreknowledge depends on, one might insist that, since believing is more basic then believing the truth, one cannot appeal to God's believing the truth as the fact on which God's foreknowledge depends: believing the truth is simply not ontologically basic enough to "carry the weight" of the soft fact in question, for it itself depends on the soft fact of God's believing.

Perhaps we can capture the heart of this response as follows. What we are looking for is an understanding of degrees of ontological basicality. Suppose we take states, events, or processes to be the ontological particles in question; then what we want to know is what it is for a state, event, or process to be more ontologically basic than another. Suppose we then accept the following account:

D6: *O* is ontologically more basic than *O'* if and only if (i) *O'* is necessarily such that whoever conceives of *O'* conceives of *O*, and (ii) *O* is not necessarily such that whoever conceives of *O* conceives of *O'*.

Given D6, we might be able to capture the last response by saying that the state of believing is ontologically more basic than the state of believing the truth, for whoever conceives of the second conceives of the first, but not vice versa.

D6 alone is not sufficient to ground this complaint against the compatibilist, for when one considers the two states of God's believing the truth and God's believing, the same response fails. Whoever conceives of God's believing the truth conceives of God's believing, and whoever conceives of God's believing conceives of God's believing the truth. Thus there is no reason to think that God's believing the truth is any less ontologically basic than His believing.

What the incompatibilist requires at this point is a generality requirement about ontological basicality; that a certain state, event or process which includes objects of type *Z* is ontologically more basic for object *z* of type *Z* only if that state, event or process is ontologically more basic for all objects of type *Z*. Since God is a person, God's believing the truth could only be as ontologically basic as believing if any person's believing the truth is as ontologically basic as believing. Since I am a person and my believing the truth is not as ontologically basic as my believing on D6, God's believing the truth is not either.

The difficulty here is in determining when individuals belong to the same type and when they do not. Surely all things considered, God is radically different from ourselves; so perhaps He ought to be classified as a type all of His own. Then His believing the truth will be as ontologically basic as His believing, whereas our believing the truth need not be as basic as our believing.

The incompatibilist might claim that no being can be allowed to be a unique member of a type. If this claim is allowed, then his desired conclusion will once again follow; for, presumably, if God is a member of some type of which there are other members, the type in question will include humans. If it does, then God's beliefs will be more basic than His believing the truth, and then His beliefs will be hard facts about the past since ours are. But there is no reason to accept such a requirement.

The proper conclusion to draw is that, even if the appeal to ontological basicality is justified, it does not show that incompatibilism is true. If God is put in the same class as mere humans, the incompatibilist conclusion follows. If His uniqueness is preserved by placing Him in a class by Himself, then the argument for incompatibilism is undermined. Further, the intuitive answer here is clear: there is nothing that is sufficiently like God for ontological purposes to be put in the same class as Him. Therefore, this last attempt on behalf of incompatibilism fails as well.

Nonetheless, the appeal to ontological basicality and ontological dependence is not justified. Consider the proposition *it was the case yesterday that it will rain tomorrow*, and suppose that this proposition is true. What it expresses today is a soft fact. If Fischer's ontological dependence criterion is acceptable, there must be some fact on which this soft fact depends. Is there? Clearly not; the only "fact" on which it depends is a future "fact", and, as pointed out in Chapter 1, there are none of these. There are fact-types and event-types of which there will be instances in the future, but there are no future facts or events. Hence the ontological dependence and basicality requirements are not justified.

This last constraint on the debate about whether God's beliefs are soft facts or not is the strongest argument of which I am aware for showing that God's beliefs in the past are hard facts, and hence against accepting the line I have taken in defending that freedom and foreknowledge are not incompatible. Since this last and strongest line of argument for the incompatibility thesis fails, I suggest that the lesson to be learned is that it is quite improbable that a good argument for incompatibilism is forthcoming.

CONCLUSION

Pike claimed that the problem he raises is about the relationship between *essential* omniscience and human freedom. We are now in a position to see that this is wrong. For if God is essentially omniscient, then whatever He believed in the past about the future *entails* that the future will be as He believes it will. Our account of accidental necessity then allows that what God believed in the past is not a fact strictly about the past; hence Plantinga is right and Pike wrong in thinking that God's beliefs must be included in that part of the history of the world that must remain constant when determining what a person has the power to do.

There would be a problem between foreknowledge and freedom if it is not possible that there be an essentially omniscient being, for then God's beliefs could not entail anything about the future. This point was reinforced by our discussion of Fischer's requirement that soft facts be parasitic on ontologically basic facts: there I suggested that this requirement only generates incompatibilism on the assumption that God is of fundamentally the same kind as we are. Now this suggestion is false if God is not essentially omniscient, for if God is only omniscient and not essentially omniscient, then even on the definition of accidental necessity I defended, God's beliefs are strictly about the past and cannot be altered. Thus in order for the version of the incompatibility thesis which rests on features of the past to be defended, it must be held that it is not possible that there is an essentially omniscient being.

We saw in Chapter 1 an argument by Swinburne intended to show that God could not know the future free actions of men. I suggested that the argument was a bad one; yet I did not claim to have shown that God knows all the future free actions of men – I only claimed that it is possible that He knows of them. There is a connection between Swinburne's claims and the incompatibility thesis; to see how, let us look again at the claims that Swinburne makes:

All the same it could happen that there was a person P having beliefs about all the future actions of free men, all of whose beliefs turned out to be true. But P could only be omniscient if in fact no man ever chose to make P's beliefs false. Yet, since the free actions of men although influenced, are not necessitated by other agents or prior states of the world, if nevertheless all of P's beliefs turned out to be true that would be a very fortunate coincidence, to say the least.

Surely a theist does not want to claim that God is omniscient in this very precarious way.[43]

Swinburne formulates the problem of freedom as a problem for the doctrine of omniscience. We have already seen that this view is mistaken. Yet, even if we can defend that God does know the future, Swinburne's worry can be recast as a worry about the doctrine of the essential omniscience of God. Just as Swinburne allows that a being might, by luck, happen to have all true beliefs about the future, perhaps such a being could just happen to know all that he believes. But, in order to be essentially omniscient, a being must be absolutely certain of what he knows in such a way that the possibility of error is completely eliminated. Besides, if there is nothing which necessitates the future free actions of men, how is it possible for any being to be absolutely certain in the required sense of what humans will do?

There is a close connection here with the last argument for the incompatibility thesis, because if it cannot be defended that God is essentially omniscient, then his beliefs count as part of the history of the world over which we have no power. Thus, in order to be able to do otherwise than we actually will do, we would have to be able to make God have a false belief. Since that is not possible given the omniscience of God, we would lack the ability to do otherwise if God is omniscient.

The task of the next chapter is, therefore, a critical one. First, we still have left the task imposed by our exceedingly minimal conclusion of the first chapter. There I merely defended that God can know some of the future actions of men; what still remains to be shown is that God can know all of the future. Also, we have the task imposed by this chapter; that of defending the doctrine of essential omniscience. We must give some indication of how God can know that which is not necessitated – such an account is critical for defending that God can be omniscient; but we must also show how God can know that which is not necessitated so that He can be absolutely certain about that which is not necessitated. Finally, we shall have to defend that in addition to having knowledge and being absolutely certain, a being can have both of these properties in every world in which He exists. To this imposing task we turn in the next chapter.

4 The Nature of God's Knowledge

A brief summary of the results so far obtained is in order at this point. We have seen that to say a being is omniscient is to say that that being justifiably believes all and only true propositions, and to say that a being is essentially omniscient is to say that that being is necessarily such that he justifiably believes all and only true propositions. Further, we have seen the failure of the arguments for the claim that there is an incompatibility between persons' having freedom and a being's having essential foreknowledge of what persons will do.

The issue left unaddressed here is how it is possible for any being to have the sort of absolute certainty necessary in order to know essentially what a free individual will do. It is not difficult to understand how justified beliefs about these occurrences can obtain, and hence how omniscience is possible; yet to foreknow essentially requires a justification inconsistent with even the minutest possibility of error. And, as we saw in the last chapter, it is necessary for a defence of the compatibility thesis that the possibility of such essential foreknowledge be maintained; for if essential foreknowledge is not possible, the account of accidental necessity presented in the last chapter would imply that God's beliefs about the future are hard facts, just as our beliefs are.

Since the implications of allowing that God's beliefs are hard facts about the past are, as we have seen, quite problematic, what is needed is a defence of the possibility of essential omniscience. Traditionally, the problematic cases regarding what is known by God have been of two kinds. First, there is empirical knowledge, the knowledge which we have through the use of our senses. Since God is immaterial, and since having the capacity to sense seems to be connected with having a body, it is initially problematic how God can know what we know empirically. Second, there is knowledge of free agents, in particular what free actions such agents will perform in the future. A defence of the doctrine of essential omniscience should account for both these issues.

A part of what I wish to defend is taken from a very important account of God's knowledge which, on its own, does not accomplish both the tasks that face us. The importance of the account is partly due to its historical significance; it is the position held by both Augustine and Aquinas, and suggested by Descartes (at times). Since this account includes certain insights which will be helpful in developing an adequate defence of the doctrine of essential omniscience, let us begin by examining it.

AN INADEQUATE ANSWER

The traditional answer to the question of God's knowledge of empirical matters (including the future actions of humans) is that there is a reversal of the explanatory schema from truth to knowledge in God's case. For us, the empirical truths help to explain our knowledge, for it is in discovering the truth that we come to have knowledge. Such is not the case for God, for Him it is his knowledge that explains truth. The traditional answer claims that God knows which hypotheses are possible by knowing his essence (hence preserving the intuition that everything, even logical truth, is absolutely dependent on God); and He knows which hypotheses are true by knowing what His will is. Contingent truth, then, is what God wills; and so God's knowledge of empirical truth is not explained by the truths which He knows. Rather, it is God's choosing to make these claims true that explains why they are true. God's knowledge of matters of fact is more akin to knowledge of what one produces than it is to sensory, empirical knowledge. As Augustine claims, 'It is not because things are what they are that God knows them, it is because he knows them that they are what they are.'[1] Aquinas comments on this text, saying:

> 'God's knowledge is the cause of things; for God's knowledge stands to all created things as the craftsman's to his products ... But a craftsman, like anyone exercising an intellectual skill, operates as a result of his own volition. So too, divine knowledge is a cause only in conjunction with divine will.'[2]

Later, Descartes echoes the same point, though the specific topic under discussion is logical rather than empirical truth. He says, in a letter to Mersenne, 'In God willing and knowing are a single thing, in such a way that by the very fact of willing something He knows it, and it is only for this reason that such a thing is true.'[3]

The tradition of casting God's knowledge of contingent truth as a sort of practical knowledge has a long and impressive tradition. God's knowledge of what sorts of claims might be true is not an instance of practical knowledge for most (though Descartes at times seems to hold that even God's knowledge of logical truth is this sort of practical knowledge). It is speculative knowledge. Such knowledge was thought to be like introspective knowledge since the possibilities in question were thought to be grounded in God's essence. I shall not discuss the issues surrounding the relationship between God and possibilities, for it does not seem to me that any problems relating to omniscience arise from these issues. If possibilities are completely dependent on God in the sense that He alone is responsible for anything which is possible, He can know possibilities through knowing what He is responsible for.[4] If the dependence is not quite so strong, there seems to be no difficulty in supposing He knows possibilities ratiocinatively – through, and only through, the operation of His Divine mind. But when the question concerns not possibility, but actuality, the knowledge is no longer speculative. It is practical knowledge, in that what is true is what God makes true.

This view of God's knowledge has implications which I think ought not to be tolerated. First, if persons have a certain sort of freedom, then God cannot be omniscient. For suppose we grant that no person is free unless no set of circumstances (apart from what he himself brings about) is sufficient to bring about the behaviour in question, i.e. unless only the person himself brings about his behaviour.[5] Now if God cannot know matters empirical unless he brings them about as a result of His will, then He cannot know what I will do in the future unless He brings it about that I do what He knows I will do. As Augustine says, it is God's willing that explains His knowing. But if I perform action A as a result of God's willing that I do A, then my doing A is brought about by something other than myself. But since no action is free unless brought about only by the agent himself, it follows that my doing A cannot be free.

It should be noted that this is not the problem of the apparent incompatibility of divine foreknowledge and human freedom; it is rather the problem of the actual incompatibility of a certain sort of divine involvement in what persons do and human freedom. Either God's involvement is such as to guarantee the resulting behaviour, or it is not. If it does guarantee the resulting behaviour, then the resulting behaviour is the product of God's will. On this option, the explanation of God's knowledge as practical knowledge holds: what occurs, occurs because of God's choices. But the practical knowledge model is upheld at the expense of human freedom, for it is what God wills that brings about the behaviour in question.

There is another sort of Divine involvement which does not violate freedom because it requires human co-operation. Just as I freely married my wife, yet not without her co-operation, so God can be involved in our lives without eliminating our freedom. However, if we take this understanding of Divine involvement, we can no longer retain the practical knowledge model of God's knowledge of contingent truths, for the truths in question are no longer simply dependent on God's will; they are also dependent on ours. Hence the following dilemma faces the practical knowledge model: either God's knowledge is really practical knowledge, in which case humans are no longer free; or humans are really free, in which case God's activity in bringing about contingent truths does not result in practical knowledge.

A defender of this view of God's knowledge has at least two possible replies here. One would be to claim that there really is no freedom in the required sense anyway, so the incompatibility in question ought not to bother us. I shall not take up a sustained criticism of this view, for my purpose here is not to defend that any sort of human freedom exists. My purpose is simply to defend that omniscience, even essential omniscience, is not incompatible with human freedom; and given that purpose, even if there is no freedom in the appropriate sense, the practical knowledge model of omniscience is one that cannot be accepted.

The second response is the one taken by Swinburne discussed in Chapter 1; it is to accept that neither God nor anyone else can foreknow free actions, and then attempt to restate the doctrine of omniscience so that this failure of foreknowledge does not imply a failure of omniscience. I argued there that his view is unacceptable and shall not repeat those arguments in this chapter. Thus the only course open to the practical knowledge interpretation of omniscience is to defend that necessitation and freedom are compatible; since my purpose is to defend the compatibility of omniscience and the sort of freedom that is incompatible with necessitation, we can leave that task for others.

In the introduction to this chapter, I pointed out that an account is needed with two characteristics: first, it must account for how God can know what we know empirically (perceptually), and second, it must account for how God can know the future free actions of humans in such a way that the possibility of essential omniscience is not eliminated. We are now in a position to see why the practical knowledge interpretation is deficient. Whereas it is quite adequate in satisfying the first constraint above, it fails in that it violates the second constraint. What is needed, then, is a way of accounting for God's knowledge of future free actions which does not make those actions dependent on God's will in the way that the practical interpretation of God's knowledge does. Let us see how such a theory is to be developed.

A MOLINIST ACCOUNT OF OMNISCIENCE

The view that I wish to defend concerning God's foreknowledge of future free actions was first developed by a sixteenth-century Jesuit priest by the name of Luis de Molina.[6] Molina was disturbed, as we are, by the requirement of the Thomistic view that freedom and necessitation are compatible. Molina's answer was to distinguish a third type of knowledge that God has. Aquinas had granted two types: God's knowledge of possibilities, and His knowledge of actualities. The first type was a speculative type of knowledge, the second a practical sort. Molina claimed that there was a third kind, which he called *scienta media*, or middle knowledge.[7] Middle knowledge, according to Molina, was the knowledge that God has of what an individual would do if placed in certain circumstances. It bears close relations to knowledge about the truth of counterfactuals, though, as we shall see later, knowledge of such truths is not identical to knowledge of true counterfactuals. As such, this type of knowledge is not purely of possibilities, for it is about what individuals would do if actual. Molina's claim was that such knowledge is not practical knowledge either; he claimed that some of these counterfactuals (the ones about free individuals) were *counterfactuals of freedom*. Since Molina took freedom to be incompatible with any sort of necessitation apart from the individual himself (as we are), it follows that middle knowledge is not practical knowledge either. Hence, for understanding God's omniscience, we must posit not only speculative and practical knowledge but middle knowledge as well.

The question we must address is how such a Molinist position is able to account for knowledge of future free actions while not implying the impossibility of essential knowledge of such actions. There are two points that must be maintained here. First, the account presented must allow that, for any moment prior to the time a certain free action is performed, God knows that that action will be done. The critical point in time for satisfying this constraint is that time preceding creation. Our account of God's omniscience must have the implication that, before God creates anything, he still knows about what He will or could create, how it will or would turn out. Initially, it is not obvious that a Molinist position can account for such knowledge, for, as I formulated the view above, it is a position about what individuals will do if placed in certain circumstances. Yet, before creation, there are no individuals other than God; so how can God know what He is doing at creation?

The second point that must be made is that, however we understand God's pre-creative knowledge, we must understand it in such a way that the future remains open after his creative activity. Since we are assuming that humans are free, what the future brings is partially up to us. For example, we cannot simply interpret God's creative activity as the instantiation of a possible world; for if any of God's creatures are truly free, they must be partially responsible for which possible world is actualised. So we cannot just say that God creates by actualising some possible world.

Our task is to capture both these requirements in a Molinistic account of middle knowledge. Let us begin with the topic of creation. I suggest that we accept:

D1:   God creates the world at $t =_{df.}$ there is a set of essences $e_1 \ldots e_n$ such that God instantiates $e_1 \ldots e_n$ at t.

D1 does not claim that God's creation of the world is the actualisation of a possible world; rather it claims that God creates by instantiating essences. What is an essence? We can define an essence as:

D2: E is an essence $=_{df.}$ E is a property which is necessarily such that (i) it is possible that something exemplify it, and (ii) it is not possible that more than one thing exemplify it.

I further suggest that we accept:

P1:   Necessarily, for every x, x has an essence.

These definitions so far imply that when God creates he makes individuals that exemplify essences. Nothing he makes lacks an essence, for there is nothing that fails to have an essence.

Since essences are properties, and properties are necessary beings, we cannot say that in creating, God creates objects with essences. If God were to create objects with essences, that might be taken to imply that at creation, God creates objects and essences. That is necessarily false, for it is not possible that essences do not exist.

We are taking as one of our assumptions that a subset of the essences which God instantiated at creation are free creatures. Given this assumption, we must distinguish between those characteristics of the world which God actualises and those characteristics the world has that are due to the creative activity of the free creatures in that world. To clarify this distinction, we can say:

D3: God actualises possible world $W =_{df.}$ (i) W is actual, and (ii) there is a set of basic actions which God performs such that God's performing them entails that W is actual.

D4: God does not actualise possible world $W =_{df.}$ either (i) God does not ordain that W is actual, or (ii) there is no set of basic actions which God performs which is such that its performance entails that W is actual.

God's ordination is to be understood as:

P2: Necessarily, God ordains that p if and only if p.

So, if a world is actual but is not actualised by God, it follows that in creating God has created free individuals. This follows given the intuitive idea that no action is basic unless performing it does not require the co-operation of other free individuals. Thus, for example, starting a war is not a basic action because, apart from free actions by other humans, no war will have been started. This intuitive idea of co-operation is captured in the definitions in the previous chapter which claimed that a basic action A is one which is performed by directly performing some action which is causally sufficient for the performance of A in normal circumstances. Since, if a person is free, there are no circumstances causally sufficient for his co-operation, our definitions imply that an action requiring co-operation by a free agent is a non-basic action. So, if a world is actual but is not actualised by God, what God has actualised is a certain range of worlds, the one which is actual being partly up to the free individuals that God has created. Let us call such a range of possible worlds a galaxy:

D5: G is a galaxy at $t =_{df.}$ G is a set of worlds such that, for any worlds W and W', W and W' are members of G at t if and only if W and W' share the same history up to and including t.

The notion of the same history is the notion appealed to in the last chapter in determining what the distinction is between hard and soft facts. Thus we can say that two worlds share the same history up to and including *t* just in case any hard fact at a time up to and including *t* in the first world is a hard fact about the same time in the second world. Given D5 and this understanding of the notion of sameness of history, we can say:

D6:   God actualises galaxy $G =_{df}$ (i) some member of *W* of *G* is actual, and (ii) the truth of (i) is compatible with God's not actualising *W*.

Affirming D1–D6, P1–P2, and that some human beings are free entails that God actualised a galaxy, but not a possible world. In actualising only a galaxy, He gave us the power to determine which member of that galaxy would be the actual world. Hence, in affirming the principles and definitions above, we satisfy the second constraint imposed above on any Molinist account: namely, that such an account must allow that the future is open. The way these definitions and principles capture this point is by implying that, if there are any free individuals, which possible world is actual is due in part to their actions of actualising it. They, of course, work in cooperation with God in this matter, and also in co-operation with each other; yet each person has the power to make a different world actual whenever they have the power to do otherwise than they actually do. Thus the second constraint, that our account leave the future open, is satisfied.

But what of the first requirement, that it be possible for God to know what will obtain even before He creates? In order to capture this constraint, it must be claimed that essences are such that, even before they are instantiated, they reveal what an instantiation of them would be like. What must be included in the above account is a version of the Molinist doctrine about counterfactuals of freedom. The term 'counterfactual' here is quite misleading; for of course, if there are such truths and God considers them in determining what world to create, some of them will not be counter to fact – God will act so that the antecedent of the conditional is true. In order to avoid misunderstanding, then, I shall refer to such conditionals as 'subjunctives of freedom'. The particular version of Molinism that I shall defend implies that each free individual's essence includes a maximal subjunctive of freedom. Thus we can accept:

P3:   Necessarily, for every essence *E* such that it is possible that an instantiation of *E* is free, an essential property of *E* is of the form *being such that some maximal subjunctive of freedom F regarding a free instantiation of E is true.*

I wish the notion of a maximal subjunctive of freedom to be understood as:

D7:   *F* is a maximal subjunctive of freedom regarding an instantiation of $E =_{df.}$ (i) *being such that F is true* is included in *E*; and (ii) where '*S*' = 'an instantiation of *E* which is free', every proposition which is a component of *F* is of the form *if S were in circumstances C at t, S would do A at t*, where (a) *C* at *t* are galactocentric, (b) there is no *C* such that it is possible that *S* is in *C* and no proposition of the form *if S were in C at t, S would do A at t* which is a component of *F*, and (c) for any act or omission of an act *A**, either *if S were in C, S would do A* at t* or *if S were in C, S would not do A* at t* is included in *F*.

D7 contains the technical notion of certain circumstances being galactocentric. The rough idea here is that we want the specification of the circumstances in the antecedent to be maximally complete regarding the history of the world in question. To say that circumstances are galactocentric is to say that, for all the worlds in the galaxy of which the actual world is a member, the circumstances contain a proposition *p* if and only if *p* is true in every member of the galaxy up to the moment in question. Putting this point more carefully, we get:

D8:   Circumstances *C* at *t* are galactocentric $=_{df.}$ for subjunctive *in C at t, S would do A at t, C* includes the property of being such that *p* is true, for every *p* such that *p* is a proposition which defines the actual galaxy at *t*, except for those propositions entailed by *S*'s doing *A* at *t*.

A bit of explanation is in order concerning the formal machinery above. P3 implies that there are true subjunctives of freedom about every free individual. The definition of a maximal subjunctive of freedom has two crucial properties. First, when the antecedent of a subjunctive is maximally specific (i.e. galactocentric by D8) regarding the history of the world, there is always a true subjunctive regarding what a person would do in such circumstances. Second, every act or omission (or the absence of the act or omission) is the consequent of some true subjunctive of the required sort.

These definitions and principles complete the Molinist account of omniscience that I wish to defend. This account satisfies the two constraints placed on any acceptable account at the beginning of this section. First it implies that the future is open if God has created any free creatures, by virtue of its stipulation that if God creates any free creatures then He does not actualise a world, but only a galaxy of worlds. Second, this account implies that before creation, God knew what would occur given any possible creative activity in which He might engage. This implication holds by virtue of P3 and D7–D8, which claim that any essence whose instantiation might be the object of God's creative activity is necessarily such that it includes a sufficiently complex collection of subjunctives of freedom so that God can know, for any possible creative act, what would follow given His performance of that act. Therefore, this account not only explains how God can have foreknowledge of free actions, it also explains how God can have essential foreknowledge of free actions. If it is acceptable, we have the sort of account needed to finish the tasks that remained from the earlier chapters. First, we will have shown that, contrary to Swinburne's claim in Chapter 1, a being can know everything about free creatures even though there is nothing that necessitates their actions. Second we will have shown that God's knowledge and beliefs held from all eternity are not hard facts about the past since His holding those beliefs both entails that what He believes is true and is explained by the truth of what He believes. The entailment point is obvious, but a word is necessary regarding the second point. God's knowledge of future free actions is not a result only of knowing His will, for what the free instantiation of an essence will do is not subject to God's will. Rather, it is the fact that an essence includes a maximal subjunctive of freedom that explains how God knows what an instantiation of that essence will do; hence it is the truth of what God believes that explains His knowledge, and not His knowledge that explains the truth of what He believes (regarding future free actions). Thus God not only foreknows what we will do, He has essential foreknowledge of our actions; and His having such essential foreknowledge bars taking his beliefs about our actions to be hard facts about the past.

What remains to be done is to defend this account as acceptable, for recently there have been strong objections raised against Molinist accounts in general.

OBJECTIONS AND REPLIES

There are two kinds of objections that might be raised against the account I have presented. The first would be to deny that there are any subjunctives of freedom. This objection may take several forms. It might be claimed that such counterfactuals are neither true nor false, and hence cannot be the objects of anyone's knowledge. Or it might be claimed that there are true subjunctives of some sort, but their truth signals that there is no freedom in such a case. The other sort of objection is to allow that there are subjunctives of freedom, but that they cannot do the explanatory work that is required by the above account. I will consider each type of objection in turn.

The Denial of Subjunctives of Freedom

One type of objection to there being subjunctives of freedom arises from the counterfactual theory of causation (hereafter referred to as 'the CTC'). Such a theory claims that there is a mutual entailment relation between causal and counterfactual claims. So, at least, when the subjunctives of freedom are also counterfactuals of freedom, those impressed with the counterfactual theory might say that if such claims are really true they are so only by virtue of signalling some sort of causal relation. There may be subjunctive truths that can be known by God, but only at the expense of freedom.

As we saw in the last chapter, though, there are several problems for any CTC. The most obvious concerns how to capture the asymmetry of causal relations. Lewis's suggestion is to note that in cases of apparent symmetrical counterfactual dependence, one of the counterfactuals will be false because worlds in which small miracles take place are closer to our world than worlds in which the entire history of the world is different from our world.[8] An alternative suggestion, one made by Swain, is that we can distinguish between symmetrical counterfactual dependencies by considering the closest worlds in which the counterfactuals are false. In one case, the falsity of one counterfactual will only require both the lack of some event and the addition of another. If these requirements are not met by the symmetrical counterfactual dependencies, then neither dependency signals a causal dependency.[9]

What I am interested in are the implications of the CTC for deliberative conditionals. The way in which deliberative conditionals enter into the present discussion of subjunctives of freedom is through God's deliberating about what sort of world to create, and what sort of actions to take after creation. Hence the deliberative conditionals in question have the form of:

(1) If S were in galactocentric circumstances C at t, S would do (or omit doing) A.

What we are attempting to evaluate is whether the truth of (4) implies that

(2) If S were in C and were to do or omit doing A, then S's being in C would be the cause of S's doing or omitting to do A.

This issue is intimately connected to the problem of asymmetry of causal dependencies, for if (1) is true, then so is:

(3) If S were not to do (or omit doing) A, S would not be in C.

Hence if the CTC is to raise a problem for Molinism, there must be some grounds on which to prefer (1) to (3) for signalling a causal dependency. And at least this much is true: the theories so far put forward do not provide such grounds. Consider, for example, any miracle theory (one version of such a theory is Lewis's theory which we considered in the last chapter) on which it is claimed that (3) is really false because of the kind of miracle it would take for S to be in C but not do A (perhaps one might claim that only a minor miracle is necessary here whereas a less minor miracle is necessary for S not to do A and not be in C – perhaps the whole history of the world would have to be different for C not to obtain). Of course, this view assumes the very causal connection which the argument we are considering is attempting to establish – there is no reason at all to think that any miracle is necessary for S to be in C and yet not do A. Such an argument begs the question against the possibility of subjunctives of freedom.

Alternatively, consider the sort of theory, such as one developed by Swain discussed in the last chapter, that allows that (3) is true, but appeals to other considerations to favour (1) rather than (3) as signalling a causal relation. Swain's view requires that, for (1) to be false, it is necessary only that some event which does occur (I am assuming here that (1) is really counter to fact), fails to occur; but for (3) to be false, not only is it necessary that some event which does occur, fails to occur, it is also necessary that some event which does not occur, occurs. But just as with Lewis's view, this presumes the causal connections that are supposed to be the result of the argument. If (1) really is a subjunctive of freedom, then for it to be false, the only event that cannot occur is that S himself is the cause of his doing A. But this cannot be the event that Swain is referring to, for as I understand the notion of agent causation (which is included in the specification of the event which must be lacking for (1) to be false), it is incompatible with the sort of causation which undermines freedom. Hence Swain's view does not support the argument against subjunctives of freedom from the CTC either.

There is a general point that should be noted here. It is usually the case that contemporary philosophers who are developing a counterfactual theory of causality, as well as those investigating the truth conditions for subjunctives in general, either restrict their investigation to deterministic worlds, or simply assume a deterministic view of this world. This assumption may be justified, for several reasons. First, there may be good arguments that determinism is true. Even if determinism is true, though, that is irrelevant here; for the purpose of my discussion is to show how God can be essentially omniscient even if some actions are anti-deterministically free. For that task, the issue of the truth or falsity of determinism does not arise.

The attractions of determinism, though, do not get to the heart of the reasons why work in this area has assumed a deterministic outlook. More to the point are the massive difficulties involved in understanding counterfactuals and other subjunctives. The immensity of these difficulties may support the use of some simplifying assumptions at the early stages of research into the issues. Thus some progress may be achievable by assuming determinism, whereas without that assumption, no progress at all can be expected. Yet if this is the reason for the assumption, we can dismiss the results of such research for our topic. It is as intuitively obvious that there are subjunctives of freedom as there are subjunctives in general; though there may be good pragmatic reasons for the simplifying assumptions of determinism in the beginning stages of research on such subjunctives, it is a logical howler of the first degree to use the results of such research as an argument that there are no subjunctives of freedom.

So there is no general problem raised by the CTC for thinking that there are subjunctives of freedom. A stronger objection is to claim that there are no true subjunctives of the relevant kind. Recently, Robert Adams has defended that subjunctives of freedom are neither true nor false. His argument is somewhat complicated, and in order to examine it we first should consider the following examples he gives of subjunctives of freedom:

(4) If David stayed in Keilah, Saul would besiege the city;

(5) If David stayed in Keilah and Saul besieged the city, then the men of Keilah would surrender David to Saul;

(6) If David stayed in Keilah, Saul would not besiege the city;

and

(7) If David stayed in Keilah and Saul besieged the city, then the men of Keilah would not surrender David to Saul.

Adams argues that all these are false by considering an argument given by Suarez for claiming that either (4) or (6), and either (5) or (7) must be true.[10] The argument claims that each is a pair of contradictories, and one or the other must be true. Adams says:

> Suarez would say that (4) and (6), and (5) and (7), respectively, are pairs of contradictories, and therefore that one member of each pair must be true. He thus affirms what has been called the law of Conditional Excluded Middle. But this is a mistake. To obtain the contradictory of a conditional proposition is not enough to negate the consequent (sic); one must negate the whole conditional, as was pointed out by Suarez's Dominican opponent, Diego Alvarez. It is true that in everyday speech we might deny (4) by asserting (6), as we may deny a proposition by asserting any belief we hold that is obviously enough inconsistent with it. But we might also deny both of them by asserting, 'If David stayed in Keilah, Saul might or might not besiege the city.'[11]

Adams then considers other ways in which, as he puts it, the truth of a subjunctive of freedom might be *grounded*.[12] First, he notes that such truths cannot be claimed to be true in the way that claims about the future are true. He says:

> Most philosophers ... have supposed that categorical predictions, even about contingent events, can be true by corresponding to the actual occurrence of the event that they predict. But propositions (4) and (6) are not true in this way. For there never was nor will be an actual besieging of Keilah by Saul, nor an actual betrayal of David to Saul by the men of Keilah, to which those propositions might correspond.[13]

Next, Adams considers the suggestion that there is a necessary connection between antecedent and consequent that explains the truth of a subjunctive of freedom. There are two possibilities here according to Adams: logical and causal necessity. Neither will work, says Adams, for 'both these suggestions are inconsistent with the assumption that

Saul's actions would have been free'.[14] Finally, Adams considers that there is a non-necessitating connection between the antecedent and consequent, perhaps by virtue of the desires, intentions, and character of the individuals in question. Adams rejects this possibility as well:

> But the basis thus offered for the truth of (4) and (5) is inadequate precisely because it is not necessitating. A free agent may act out of character, or change his intentions, or fail to act on them. Therefore the propositions which may be true by virtue of correspondence with the intentions, desires and character of Saul and the men of Keilah are not (4) and (5) but
>
> (8) If David stayed in Keilah, Saul would *probably* beseige the city.
>
> (9) If David stayed in Keilah and Saul besieged the city, the men of Keilah would *probably* surrender to Saul.
>
> (8) and (9) are enough for David to act on, if he is prudent; but they will not satisfy the partisans of middle knowledge. It is part of their theory that God knows infallibly what definitely would happen, and not just what would probably happen or what free creatures would be likely to do.[15]

Presumably, these are the only possiblities that Adams sees for showing that subjunctives of freedom are either true or false. In summary, Adams' view then is that there is no good argument for thinking that subjunctives of freedom are either true or false. The law of Conditional Excluded Middle is false, middle knowledge is not foreknowledge, necessary connections between antecedent and consequent violate freedom, and non-necessitating connections at best show that (8) and (9) are true, not (4) and (5). Hence, since there are no other possibilities, there is no good reason to think that subjunctives of freedom are either true or false.

Adams' arguments deserve closer inspection. He first dismisses Suarez's view by claiming that the law of Conditional Excluded Middle is false. He does not give any counter-examples to that law, but refers to some that have been given in the literature.[16] The examples that are used are of the following kind. First, it is claimed to be true that:

(10) If Reagan and Chernenko had been compatriots, then either Reagan would have been a Russian or he would not.

Yet, it is claimed, neither of the following is true:

(11) If Reagan and Chernenko had been compatriots, then Reagan
     would have been a Russian;
(12) If Reagan and Chernenko had been compatriots, then Reagan
     would not have been a Russian.

I do not find examples of this sort especially compelling, for it is easy
to confuse whether either (11) or (12) is true with whether and how one
might determine which of the two is true. I have no idea which is true;
but that is an epistemological point, not a metaphysical one – and it is a
metaphysical point that needs to be established to show that neither of
the two is true.

A perhaps more likely explanation of the rejection of the law of
Conditional Excluded Middle is the particular semantics that are
accepted for subjunctive conditionals. Such conditionals have truth-
values determined with reference to possible worlds ranked by certain
standards of similarity. A conditional is true, on these semantics, if in
the most similar possible world in which the antecedent is true, the
consequent is true as well. Such a conditional is false in all other cases.

What these semantics leave open is the possibility that two worlds
are tied on similarity standards. The question then arises: what happens
if two worlds in which the antecedent obtains are tied, and yet the
consequent obtains in one of those worlds and not the other? The
answer is obvious: we have then a violation of the law of conditional
excluded middle.

I do not wish to defend that the law in question is true; my point is
only that it might be a consideration of the standard semantics for such
conditionals that brings one to the admission that the law is false rather
than a consideration of particular examples. For consideration of
particular examples here leaves undetermined whether it is the epistemological inability to tell which claim is true, or the needed metaphysical
conclusion that neither is true.

In any case, Suarez's argument is inconclusive in the absence of a
defence of the law in question, so Adams is at least correct in holding
that we have no compelling argument here for the truth of the claims in
question. Let us then examine Adams' necessitation arguments: the
arguments which claim that if the claims are not true in virtue of a
necessary connection between antecedent and consequent, then only a
probabilistic consequent follows; and if the claims are true in virtue of a
necessary connection, then freedom is violated.

Adams is surely right that if the antecedent *causally* necessitates the
consequent, then on our assumptions any action referred to in the

consequent will not be a free action. But what of logical necessity? Adams claims that this sort of connection is also incompatible with freedom. Our discussion in the last chapter has shown that this claim is false. If God knows what I will do, there is an entailment relation between his knowledge and my action; yet my action can still be free. The appeal to God's knowledge here is not necessary: if anyone knows what I will do, that entails that I perform the action in question. Hence Adams is wrong in saying that logical necessitation is incompatible with freedom.

On the other hand, Adams is right when he says that logical necessitation is not an adequate explanation of the truth of subjunctive conditionals, for there are many subjunctive conditionals which are true and yet do not involve logical necessitation. One can truly say that had I overslept today, I would have been late without implying that my oversleeping entails my being late. So even if logical necessitation does not violate freedom, it is not the sort of connection that can explain how subjunctives of freedom are true.

The other part of the necessitation argument concerns what is true if the connection is non-necessitating. Instead of *if A then B*, Adams claims that all we are left with is *if A then probably B*. The sort of non-necessitating connection that Adams considers is one that obtains by virtue of the character, intentions, and desires of the person in question. He then claims that at best the probabilistic subjunctive is true because a free agent may act out of character, change his intentions, or fail to act on them. So with regard to Saul and the besieging of Keilah, only (8) and (9) can be true, not (4) or (5).

The precise structure of this argument is not perfectly clear but the crucial premise is:

(13) If David had stayed in Keilah, Saul might have acted out of character.

Further the position under attack is:

(14) (4) and (5) are true in virtue of Saul's character.

The difficulty with this argument is that both premises could use a bit more clarity. Whatever else (14) may imply, I think Adams means it to imply:

(14′) Necessarily, given Saul's character, (4) and (5) are true.

Adams wishes to infer from (13) and (14′) that (4) and (5) are not true. Does this claim follow?

Well, that depends on how we read (13). We might read it as follows:

(13′) It is possible that (David stays in Keilah and Saul acts out of character).

This reading, however, does not show that (4) and (5) are false; it only shows that, in some possible world, they are false. In other words, all that follows from (13′) and (14′) is that the following are false:

(15) Necessarily, if David were to stay in Keilah, Saul would beseige the city,

and

(16) Necessarily, if David were to stay in Keilah and Saul were to beseige the city, the men of Keilah would surrender David to Saul.

The only way I can see to make the argument valid is to read the 'might' in (13) as a counterfactual 'might'. Thus, for example, in the case considered earlier in which it is supposed that the law of Conditional Excluded Middle fails, we can say Reagan might or might not have been Russian if he and Chernenko had been compatriots; and the intended reading here of 'might' is the sort which implies that this case involves a violation of the law of Conditional Excluded Middle.

This reading of (13) would imply, with (14′), that both (4) and (5) are false; however, there is no reason at all for thinking that, in this sense of 'might', Saul might act out of character. There are several readings in which it is true that Saul might act out of character: we might mean that it is possible that he so act, or that he has the power to so act, or even that there is some chance that he will so act. But none of these generates the conclusion that both (4) and (5) are false – in fact, it seems intuitively obvious that each of these readings of (13) is quite compatible with the truth of both (4) and (5). The only reading which does generate the required conclusion is one which stands in need of defence. How such a defence could go, save by implication from the falsity of both (4) and (5), is hard to see. The temptation here is to think that if this is the reading of (13) that Adams intends, the reason he thinks it is true is precisely because he thinks that both (4) and (5) are false. Of course, he cannot then use that reading of (13) to argue that both are false.

None the less, even if no argument is forthcoming here that neither (4) nor (5) are true, Adams is still right that (14) is false, as long as it is assumed that any plausible reading of (14) entails (14′), for (14′) is clearly false. For there is no contradiction implied by assuming that

Saul's character is as it is and yet both (4) and (5) are false. Hence if Adams has (14') in mind as the interpretation of (14), then the argument he gives, though a bad one, is not essential to showing that (14) is false.

Yet, if what Adams has in mind by (14) is (14') (or something that entails (14')), it begins to look very much as if Adams is really asking for some indication of which additional components are to be added to the antecedent of a subjunctive conditional to turn it into a true entailment. So, perhaps, the only sort of response here that would satisfy Adams would be a reductionistic response: what must be shown is that subjunctive conditionals are just disguised instances of entailments.

Even more reductionistic elements appear in Adams' position when we consider the only other attempt Adams considers at grounding the truth of subjunctives of freedom. Adams asserts that (some) philosophers have granted that claims about the future can be true by virtue of corresponding to the actual occurrences of the event they predict. Adams then perfunctorily dismisses this attempt (I take it that the attempt is to say that the claims are true by virtue of some sort of correspondence relation to the world) by claiming that middle knowledge is not simply foreknowledge.

Now of course middle knowledge is not simply foreknowledge; but why must it be? A plausible answer is that Adams is imposing reductionistic requirements here again: if one is to explain how (4) and (5) are true by appealing to some sort of correspondence relation, that relation will have to be between the propositions in question and some event which has occurred, is now occurring, or will occur. None of these is plausible, so subjunctive conditionals cannot be grounded in this fashion.

I wish to return to this argument later, for I think that Adams' charge can be answered. But before answering the charge, let us consider the conclusion that Adams wishes to draw from his purported demonstration of the inability to ground the truth of subjunctives of freedom. He claims, 'I trust that it is clear by this point that there is reason to doubt the possibility of middle knowledge.'[17]

Adams seems to suggest, then, that in the absence of a ground for the truth of (4) and (5), there is reason to doubt that middle knowledge is possible. We must be careful in drawing conclusions of this sort, for it has not yet been shown that there needs to be a ground for the truth of (4) and (5). For example, suppose someone claimed that proposition (4) is true because if David had stayed, Saul would have besieged. Does this explanation state a *ground* for the truth of (4)? I should think not; but perhaps it is the only answer that can be given for explaining the ground of the truth of any proposition. Until Adams enlightens us as to what would count as a ground and what would not, it is not clear that the simple explanation above is not all that is needed; and it is especially unclear why any reason for doubt has been indicated even if all Adams' arguments were sound.

On the other hand, there is good reason not to be worried by Adams' charges here; and we can see our way out of any difficulty by considering more closely the attempt to ground the truth of (4) and (5) by some sort of correspondence to the actual world. Adams rejects such an account by reminding us that middle knowledge is not foreknowledge. Of course, that is true; but we can gain some insight into how to defend the possibility of middle knowledge by noting how Adams suggests that claims about the future are true. He says that 'categorical propositions can be true by corresponding to the actual occurrence of the event that they predict'.[18] Such an account of the truth of propositions about the future accords well with the position I defended in the last chapter about the ontological priority of the present: since it is what is occurring now that is most truly real, any contingent proposition that is true must be true in virtue of some relation to some "now" or other. Such a position generates simple explanations for the truths about the past and future. There are truths about the past because there was a time in the past at which some particular event, state or process, etc was "present". Further, there are truths about the future because there will be such "present" events at some future time.[19]

Now, of course, one cannot explain the truths of subjunctives of freedom in exactly the terms used to explain the past or future; to do so would entail that such subjunctives are either truths about the past or future. The same is trivially true about both the past and the future: one cannot explain truth about the future in terms of the past; one cannot explain past truths in terms of the future; one can only explain past and future truths in terms of the (then) present. Can we then explain the truth of subjunctives of freedom in terms of some "present" or other? Easily; take the claim that if *S* were in *C*, *S* would do *A*. This claim asserts that if there were a (present) time at which *S* was then in *C*, at that time *S* would (then) do *A*.

The lesson to be learned here is that if we impose the sorts of restrictions that Adams imposes on counterfactuals, on claims about either the past or future, there will be no such truths either. If one becomes sceptical that there are truths about the future, and insists on a clarification of what makes these claims true, all that can be offered is *what the present will be like.* If the objector then insists that one has begged the question by appealing to the reality of the future already, there is not much more that can be said. Similarly with regard to the past; if one insists on a clarification of what makes claims about the past true, all that can be offered is *what the present was like.* And again, if the objector insists that one has begged the question by appealing to the reality of the past, there is not much more to be said. Finally, the same goes for claims about subjunctives of freedom. If the objector insists on a clarification of what makes these claims true, all that can be offered is *what the present would be like,* or *would have been like.* Once more, if the objector insists that one has begged the question by appealing to what is in question in the first place, there is not much more that can be said. What ought to be inferred from all this is that such begging the question objections need not be taken that seriously. If the reality of the past and future goes down the drain with the subjunctives of freedom, so much the worse for worries about subjunctives of freedom.

Note that this account that employs the ontological priority of the present accords well with a sort of account that is plausible regarding possibility claims and claims about possible worlds. If it is true that it is possible that p, that means that in some possible world it is true that p. But are we committed to the reality of possible worlds to "ground" the truth of possibility claims? No, for if we accept the ontological priority of the present, we can say that a possible world is *a way this world might have been.* The referent of 'this world' in that proposition can be construed in terms of the collection of things that really exist and the total history of "present" moments. Those objects might have had different characteristics than they in fact had, have, or will have; thus, a possible world can be explained in terms of some way actual objects might have been at some "present" moment or other.

Further, note that Adams' worry about subjunctives of freedom being inexplicable in terms of the future could equally well apply to possibility claims, for after all many possibility claims are such that no actual event ever has or will occur to make them true. But this fact should not cause us to worry that no possibility claim is ever true; it should merely prompt us to search for an explanation of how the truth of such claims is parasitic on the present in virtue of being parasitic on this world as a whole. In claiming that a possible world is just another way this world might have been, we have just the account we are looking for.

There is one last objection that one might think that Adams is making, though he does not do so explicitly. One might think that subjunctives of freedom are really shortened ways of expressing probabilistic subjunctives. Thus one may think that (4) and (5) are not strictly true, though we accept them because they are shortened versions of (8) and (9) (the same as (4) and (5) with the addition of a probability operator governing the consequent). So for any apparently true subjunctive of freedom of the form *if S were in C, S would do A*, one might claim that what is really true is only *if S were in C, then probably S would do A*.

The first point to note is that ordinarily we do not talk in this way. We make claims about others whom we take to be free in the appropriate sense, and we do not qualify the consequent with a probability operator. Further, there are conditions under which we would rightly reject this translation of what we actually say. For example, suppose I said that if my car were to break down today, I would be angry. Suppose also that my friend Jim, not believing me, intends to show me that I am wrong; so he manipulates nature (in this case, he ruins my car) in order to bring about the truth of the antecedent of that conditional. My car then breaks down, but I do not get angry.

Note what we would say about such a case. Jim would surely be correct in claiming that what I had claimed was false: it is false that if my car were to break down, I would be angry. However, if we translate my assertion along the lines suggested above ('if my car were to break down today, then I would probably be angry'), we cannot say that what I said was false on the basis of Jim's little experiment. Suppose Jim had followed me in his car to see my reactions; upon discovering my lack of anger, he leaps from his car exclaiming, 'See!, I knew you were wrong!' I would be wrong to suggest that I had been right none the less, for it is still quite probable that I be angry even though I in fact am not.

Observe that, in the above case, the experiment Jim sets up is just the sort that scientists set up to see if those counterfactuals implied by causal claims are true. Unless one is a complete sceptic about such experiments, it ought to be granted that such experiments do reveal whether a counterfactual or subjunctive is true or not. Further, once this is granted, it is clear that Jim's experiment shows the original assertion to be false; since it does not show that the alternative, probabilistic, interpretation of the statement is false, that account is faulty.

Thus I suggest that the objections to the existence of subjunctives of freedom, the one based on the CTC and Adams' objections, fail. If such statements are true, they can include free actions in the consequent. Further, there is no good objection to thinking that they are true. Adams' alternative is clearly unacceptable, and his claims that there is no ground for explanation for the truth of such subjunctives is false. The truth of such subjunctives can be explained in the same way as the truth of claims about the past, future, and other possible worlds can: namely, by the ontological priority of the present. Finally, even if there were no such explanation available, it does not follow that there is any reason to doubt that such statements have a truth-value. At some point, we must run out of explanations; when we get to that point it does not follow that we are unjustified in starting at that point.

Are Subjunctives of Freedom Useless?

However, there are more serious objections to the view I am defending than the above. One of the constraints that I have placed in my account is that God be able to know the truth of subjunctives of freedom before creation. There are three strong objections to this view.

The Circularity Objection

The first objection claims that even if there are true subjunctives of freedom, they are not true at any time which they could be of use to God in contemplating what to create. This objection has been raised most forcefully by Anthony Kenny.[20] Let us begin by considering his formulation which assumes the possible worlds semantics that I have been employing for determining the truth-value of a subjunctive. Kenny says:

> Prior to God's decision to actualize a particular world those counter-factuals cannot yet be known: for their truth-value depends ... on which world is the actual world. It is not simply that God's knowledge of these counterfactuals cannot be *based on* a decision which has to be taken *subsequent* to knowledge of them ... The problem is that what makes the counterfactuals true is not yet there at any stage at which it is undecided which world is the actual world ... The difficulty is simply that if it is to be possible for God to know which world he is actualizing, then his middle knowledge must be logically prior to his decision to actualize; whereas if middle know-

ledge is to have an object, the actualization must already have taken place. As long as it is undetermined which action an individual human being will take it is undetermined which possible world is the actual world – undetermined not just epistemologically, but metaphysically.[21]

According to Kenny, the problem is that, in the possible worlds semantics, the subjunctives in question cannot be true early enough to aid God in creation. Thus the conclusion of Kenny's argument is that God cannot have middle knowledge when deciding which world to create.

Kenny's objection rests on a simple confusion. He claims that what an account like mine must posit is that there are true subjunctives of freedom before the actualisation of any world by God. The confusion is that it is simply not possible that there is no actual world; though it is possible that the actual world is one in which God has not (yet) created anything. But that is quite a different matter from there being no world at all. Kenny wishes to claim that subjunctives in question lack a truth value until some world is actual. That can be granted; without an actual world, there would be no truths at all. All that shows, however, is that it is not possible that there fails to be an actual world, for it is simply not possible that there fails to be some true propositions.

My point is simple. As long as possible worlds are understood in terms of propositions, and propositions are bivalent truth bearers (every proposition is exclusively either true or false), then it is impossible that there is no actual world. Further, since there are necessary beings such as essences, numbers, and God, the actual world must include such residents; and, according to the definitions presented earlier, the subjunctives of freedom are included in essences. Hence, since it is impossible for there to be a time at which there are no essences, it is also impossible that there is a time (even before creation) at which the truth of the subjunctives of freedom is not given. What is not given, of course, is which collection of essences God will instantiate; the mistake Kenny makes is confusing the idea of the material stuff of the physical universe with the notion of an actual world which is a quite abstract notion. Once this confusion is eliminated, the objection disappears.

The Problem of Deliberative Conditionals

The second objection is due to Adams and is directed against the Molinist position on the use of subjunctives of freedom by God in determining what to create and what not to create. To employ such subjunctives, God would have to know the truth of a class of deliberative conditionals. Adams argues that there is a problem for the standard semantics for deliberative conditionals. The propositions in question have the following form:

(17) If *S* were to do *x*, then *y* would happen,

and the standard semantics for such claims is:

(S17) Any world where *S* does *x* and *y* happens is closer to the actual world than any world in which *S* does *x* and *y* does not happen.

Adams first notes that this semantics makes the explanation of (17) appear circular:

> According to the possible worlds explanation, (whether (17) is true) depends on whether the actual world is more similar to some world in which I do x and y happens than to any world in which I do x and y does not happen. That in turn seems to depend on which world is the actual world. And which world is the actual world? That depends in part on whether I do x. Thus the truth of ('if I do x, then y would happen') seems to depend on the truth or falsity of its antecedent.[22]

None the less, Adams grants that there is a way to avoid this problem for normal deliberative conditionals; the point of his criticism, though, is that the way the problem is avoided in normal cases will not help when the conditionals are the Molinist ones God employs in deciding what to create. His solution for normal deliberative conditionals is given as follows:

> There is, I presume, a large class, K, of possible worlds that are more similar to some world in which I do x and y happens than to any world in which I do x and y does not happen. According to the possible worlds theory the truth of (17) depends on the actual world being some member of K, but not on which member of K it is. In asserting (17) in the context of deliberation I commit myself, in effect, to the view that the actual world is a member of K and that its membership in K does not depend on which I choose of the alternatives among which I am deliberating.[23]

The point of Adams' discussion of deliberative conditionals is, first, to show how ordinary deliberative conditionals must be construed, but second, to argue that this rescue attempt does not work in the context of God's deliberation about what to create. He considers a deliberative conditional such as

(18) If God created Adam and Eve, there would be more moral good than evil in the history of the world,

and says,

> Similarly there is a class, K*, of possible worlds that are more similar to some world in which God creates Adam and Eve and there is more moral good than moral evil in the history of the world than to any world in which God creates Adam and Eve and there is not more moral good than moral evil in the history of the world. The truth of (18) depends on the actual world being some member of K*, according to the possible worlds theory. But how can the actual world's membership in K* have been settled earlier in the order of explanation than God's decision whether to create Adam and Eve, or some other free creatures, or none?[24]

This objection is quite puzzling. Adams claims that there is an insoluble problem for deliberative conditionals prior to God's decision to create, but that there is no analogous problem for ordinary deliberative conditionals. There are two possibilities that I can see for understanding the first of these two claims, but only the first is compatible with Adams' second claim; the second way of understanding him is not.

On the first interpretation, Adams is guilty of the same confusion that undermined Kenny's circulatory objection to subjunctives of freedom. In other words, Adams may think that, until God creates, there literally is no actual world, and no galaxy of worlds smaller than the entire set of all possible worlds which is actual; hence 'the actual world's membership in K* could not be 'settled earlier in the order of explanation' than God's decision to create.

We have seen that this is a confusion; it is impossible that there be no actual world. Further, even if the galaxy of worlds prior to creation included all possible worlds, that would not prevent the truth of subjunctives of freedom. For there is an actual world even before creation, and the actual world contains essences which include subjunctives of freedom. Hence, if God were considering whether to create Adam and Eve, He would have to consider all the possible total circumstances He might create at the same time and then consider the properties of the various essences in question. Such a procedure would inform Him as to what would occur at the first instant of time, and analogous considerations would inform Him concerning possible histories of the world. Such consideration would then inform Him of the connections between creating Adam and Eve and the total amount of good and evil in the history of the world. So, if this interpretation of Adams' worry about deliberative conditionals is correct, we need not be bothered by the objection.

There is another possible worry about deliberative conditionals. However, it cannot be the worry that Adams has in mind. For, as we shall see, it applies equally to God's considerations prior to creation and to ordinary deliberative conditionals. This worry concerns the features of worlds that can be appealed to in determining the similarity relations between them. One might think, for example, that two worlds are most similar when they share exactly the same history (in the sense defined by the notion of a hard fact from the last chapter) up to a certain moment. In the context of deliberation concerning (17), the moment in question would be that at which one will either make the antecedent true by doing x or false by not doing it. It might be thought then that any two worlds which share the same history up to the point in question would be as similar to each other as any two worlds can be on any plausible construal of which similarity conditions are relevant.

Regarding that point in time at which God creates, the following difficulty arises. If worlds are maximally similar by sharing the same history, up to creation there are just too many such worlds to determine whether (17) is true or not. For there is not only a possible world in which S does x and y happens, there is also a possible world in which S does x and y does not happen (unless, of course, (17) is a necessary truth). Further, there also are two worlds of this sort which share the same history.

Now consider Adams' solution for normal deliberative conditionals. He claims that there is a class K of worlds which must be more similar to a world in which S does x and y occurs than to any world in which S does x and y does not occur. Yet, whatever world is actual, it is one which, by hypothesis, shares the same history with a world in which S does x and y occurs and with a world in which S does x and y does not occur, when we are considering God's deliberations prior to creation. Hence, whichever member of K the actual world is, it will be no more similar to a world in which y does not occur than to a world in which y does occur. Therefore, prior to God's creative activity, the similarity relations are not determinate enough to allow that deliberative conditionals are true.

One might think that this dilemma could be avoided by claiming that one must also allow causal laws to be part of the relevant similarity conditions. Thus, if there is a causal relation between S's doing x and y's happening, then no world with the same history as another in which that causal relation is absent can be as close to the latter world as one in which the history is the same and the causal laws are the same.

This appeal to causal laws will be of no help here, for the subjunctive conditionals which are under consideration here do not involve causal or logical connections at all; they are conditionals like the following: If God were to create Adam and Eve, they would fall. If the fall in question is to be freely done, there had better not be a causal connection between antecedent and consequent. Hence appeals to causal laws cannot eliminate the problem that Adams raises.

This difficulty is no more serious a problem for God's deliberations before creation than for ordinary conditionals. What is true is that there is less of a problem for deliberative conditionals *which are true in virtue of a causal relation between antecedent and consequent* than for deliberative conditionals concerning free actions. Consider again conditionals such as (18), which claims that if God were to create Adam and Eve, there would be more moral good than evil in the world. Such a conditional does not signal any sort of causal connection between antecedent and consequent; hence the problem for similarity of worlds arises which was discussed above. But the pre-creative dimension of that problem is not central to it; to see this consider

(19) If I were to receive a job offer from Harvard at triple my present salary, I would take the job.

Presumably, I would have the power to accept or reject such an offer were one to come, thus there is no causal necessitation which accounts for the truth of (19). Therefore, there are two worlds, both sharing the same history as well as causal and logical laws, one in which I take the job and one in which I do not. If there is nothing to similarity except sameness of history and identity of causal and logical laws, then there is no choosing which of the worlds in question is more similar to the actual world. On the standard semantics, that implies that (19) is not true.

We should not think of this problem as indicative of the view that there are true subjunctives of freedom, for that is to put the cart before the horse. The standard semantics are to be developed so as to account for those conditionals which are intuitively true; we are not to develop a semantics which eliminates intuitive truths and then argue that what are intuitive truths really must not be true at all. It is well known that there are serious problems with specifying which similarity relations are relevant on the standard semantics and which are not; even if we could not give an account of the standard semantics regarding which deliberative conditionals are true and which are not, the proper conclusion should be, not that the affirmation of subjunctives of freedom is problematic on the above grounds, but that the standard semantics still has a way to go to be free of troublesome counter-examples.

Our account of subjunctives of freedom provides an explanation of the truth-value of deliberative conditionals which lack any sort of causal or logical connection between antecedent and consequent, though it is not clear whether this explanation is compatible with the standard semantics for subjunctive conditionals. The truth-value of such conditionals can be explained by the similarity relations between possible worlds, as long as it is noted that not only the history of the worlds count but also the natures of the individuals whose potential actions are under consideration. Thus, we might say, a deliberative conditional is true by virtue of the history of the world and the nature or essence of the person acting. The particular feature of this account that explains the truth-value of deliberative conditionals is that every such conditional is about some individual whose essence has properties of the form *being such that a certain subjunctive of freedom is true.*

The issue regarding whether deliberative conditionals can be explained by the standard semantics turns on whether these properties supervene on, or are explainable by, more fundamental characteristics of the essences in question. Defenders of the standard semantics must hold that these properties are dependent on more fundamental features of the essences in question. If they do not hold this view, there will be some subjunctive conditionals which have a truth-value which cannot be explained by the standard semantics, for then it will be possible for two worlds to be exactly alike (apart from the subjunctively conditional elements of the essences which are instantiated in those worlds) on all relevant grounds of similarity and yet one world is such that it is the world which would obtain were certain circumstances actual. If this were possible, the standard semantics would be conclusively refuted.

However, it is not clear that we have such a strong objection to the standard semantics for it is not clear that the subjunctives in question cannot have a truth-value explicable by more fundamental features of the essences in question. I know of no argument stating that this view is true, so I do not include it as a component of the theory being defended; but it is not clearly objectionable and should not be rejected either.

We can see that the problem of deliberative conditionals is not a problem for the Molinist account presented here. At best, the problem is one for the standard semantics for subjunctive conditionals. Yet it is not even clear that deliberative conditionals undermine the standard semantics, for defenders of the standard semantics may find refuge in the view that subjunctives of freedom supervene on, or are explained by, more fundamental features of the essences in question. If these subjunctives are not explainable by anything more fundamental, we should conclude that Molinism is faulty. Rather, the proper conclusion to draw would be that the standard semantics is unable to account for the truth of all subjunctive conditionals. In any case, we need not balk at the present theory on the basis of considerations regarding deliberative conditionals.

On the Failure of the Law of CEM

It seems to me that neither Adams' nor Kenny's objections that impute some sort of circularity to the Molinist view which I am defending count against that view. There is one other objection that might be raised which we need to consider, and it arises from the objections we considered earlier to the law of Conditional Excluded Middle (CEM). If that law is false, it might be thought that one of the aims of such a Molinistic account fails to be satisfied. For part of the motivation for Molinism is to account for *how God knows what He is doing* at creation. According to Molinism, He knows what He is doing by knowing the truth of certain subjunctives.

Yet if the law of CEM does not hold isn't it true that God cannot know which possible world is actual? Take any case in which that law does not hold, so that A does not counterfactually imply either B or *not-B*, but it does imply their disjunction. Since at most one of B or *not-B* can be true, wouldn't there be some indeterminacy in God's mind about which world would obtain, the one including B or the one including *not-B*, if God were to make a world including A?

The conclusion does not follow, for the failure of the law of CEM would undermine our account only if the law fails regarding conditionals with maximally specified antecedents. It is well known that a counterfactual of the form $A - \rangle B$ can be false and yet $A\&C - \rangle B$ be true. Further, even in cases where neither $A - \rangle B$ nor $A - \rangle$ *not-B* are true, it can be that, for some C, $A\&C \rightarrow B$ is true. What must be shown, instead of that law of CEM being false, is that the law is false regarding maximally specified antecedents.

Further, it is not implausible to think that any violations of the law of CEM are only regarding more limited antecedents. Consider again (11) which claims that had Reagan and Chernenko been compatriots, Reagan would have been Russian. The claim, it will be remembered, is that neither this nor (12), the claim that had Reagan and Chernenko been compatriots, Reagan would not have been Russian, is true. I have already asserted that this example, and other proposed counter-examples to the law, are less than compelling; however, let us for the moment grant that we have a counter-example here. It does not follow, even if (11) and (12) are false, that there is not another counterfactual including in its antecedent the antecedent of (11) and (12), which is true and has either the consequent of (11) or (12) as its consequent. For example, it might be true that if Reagan had not been in America, he would have been born in New Zealand. This would be true if Reagan's father had been offered two jobs a month before his birth, one of them being in New Zealand, and the others at his actual birthplace. The same sort of scenario might obtain for Chernenko: had he not been born in Russia, he would have been born in New Zealand, for his parents may have considered leaving Russia, and would have gone to New Zealand had they left. In such a case, at least this counterfactual is true: had Reagan not been born in America and Chernenko in Russia, they would have been compatriots. It is also true that had both Reagan and Chernenko been born elsewhere such that their births resulted in their being compatriots, Reagan would not have been Russian. Hence it does not follow that there is any difficulty for God to know what He is doing at creation by virtue of knowing which subjunctives are true, even if the law of Conditional Excluded Middle does not hold. It is only necessary that for every violation of the law of CEM there is another subjunctive with a complex antecedent, including the antecedent of the case which has violated the law and identical consequents, such that the more complex subjunctive is true.

I submit then that considerations concerning the law of CEM do not give any reason to doubt the adequacy of the account I have presented. First, it is not clear that that law is false, for any particular counter-example to that law is indeterminate regarding whether it is our inability to know which of the two propositions in question is true or whether it is that neither really is true. A plausible response to such a claim is that one is confusing a simple subjunctive ($A \rightarrow B$) with another subjunctive with a more complicated antecedent $(A\&C \rightarrow B)$ for which the law holds. The Reagan example above may be a good illustration of this sort of possible confusion; one thinks that either (11) or (12) is true because one thinks that there is some complicated story about what each of Reagan's and Chernenko's parents would have done to bring about births in other countries. Yet this way of rescuing the claim that there are counter-examples to the law of CEM plays into the hands of a defender of Molinism; for the Molinist does not need the law of CEM, he only needs any indeterminacy resulting from a violation of that law to be inessential. Such indeterminacy is clearly inessential when there is a more complicated antecedent for which the law holds.

CONCLUSION

I conclude then that a Molinist account of omniscience satisfies the constraints placed on an acceptable account of omniscience. Molinism accounts for how God can know without the object of knowledge being necessitated, and thus how God can know what truly free individuals will do. Further, it explains omniscience in such a way that it is possible for a being to be essentially omniscient; hence, since God is maximally perfect, He is essentially omniscient. Finally, such an account explains how God knew what He was doing at creation. By knowing which galaxies He might "travel to" by instantiating different collections of essences and by knowing which world would result from each set of "travel plans", God knew at creation what would (perhaps freely) result from each different possible creative activity. Then, simply by knowing what His will is, He could know what He would create, and know what would result. Thus, knowing the possible results as well as knowing His own will explains how God can know, and know essentially, the entirety of the future without determining it.

Strong objections have been lodged against Molinism, but I have asserted that these do not raise problems for the Molinist account I am defending. Many of these objections rest on the clearly false assumption that before God created the world, no possible world (or galaxy) was actual. Others rest on clearly unreasonable demands as to how the truth of subjunctives of freedom must be grounded; and there are others still which improperly infer that if a subjunctive is true, it must be true by virtue of a causal (or stronger, logical) relation between antecedents and consequent. Since all these objections are not telling against Molinism, I conclude that Molinism provides a proper explanation of omniscience which satisfies all the constraints that we have seen are necessary.

5 Omniscience, Omnipresence, Immutability and Timelessness

INTRODUCTION

Recently, there has been a considerable amount of discussion about the relationship between the doctrine of omniscience and other doctrines of classical theism. Kretzmann has argued that omniscience, in particular knowing what time it is, is incompatible with immutability; for if a being knows what time it is at one moment and knows what time it is at another moment, then that being has changed in some respect.[1] Another central area of concern has been the doctrine of timelessness and its relation to the doctrine of omniscience. Several philosophers have argued that if God is outside time, He cannot know that it is now Friday, 1 June, for example.[2]

In certain views of God, these problems are of utmost importance. Those of a Platonic tradition, to whom the mere fact of change signals imperfection, must be able to reconcile omniscience with immutability. Or again, those for whom the doctrine of timelessness is a device for solving the apparent incompatibility between foreknowledge and freedom, must find a way to show that God can be omniscient and yet timeless (or find some other way out of the problem they perceive between freedom and foreknowledge).

In our context, these issues are less pressing, and it is for this reason that I have left them till now. First, I see no reason to think that changeability implies imperfection; hence the concern over the cotenability of the doctrines of immutability and omniscience is not critical. There is sufficient ground for thinking that God's character and intentions are stable, but the classical doctrine of immutability implies much more than this sort of stability. Further, it is the additional elements beyond stability of intention and character which give rise to the compatibility question between omniscience and immutability. Finally, since we have seen that there is no special need for a doctrine of timelessness in order to avoid the problem of freedom and foreknowledge, some sort of argument will have to be constructed for the doctrine of timelessness to raise difficulties for the doctrine of omniscience defended here; for the traditional motivations are not compelling. Apart from such a defence of the timelessness doctrine, any apparent conflict between timelessness and omniscience can be resolved simply by abandoning the timelessness doctrine. My point is that, since the motivations for timelessness and immutability doctrines in a form which raises the issue of compatibility with omniscience are not compelling, reconciling the doctrine of omniscience with the doctrine of timelessness and immutability is not a requirement for completing the task of this work. If there is an incompatibility, there is at least a presumption that the doctrines of timelessness and immutability should be given up rather than the doctrine of omniscience; for, as I have attempted to argue, the motivations for a doctrine of omniscience are strong indeed.

None the less, it is an interesting question how much of the classical conception of God can be maintained. Given that this conception has been perceived to be incompatible with the doctrine of omniscience (a perception, I might add, that will remain undiminished given the theory of omniscience presented here), it is not inappropriate that we consider these issues here.

The timelessness doctrine claims that God is eternal, not in the sense that He is everlasting but rather that He is not in time at all. To say that a being is everlasting is to say that such a being has an existence of unlimited duration; but to say that a being is eternal in the sense required for the timelessness doctrine is to say that it is a mistake to think of that being's existence as involving the concept of duration at all. To mark the distinction between these two senses of eternal, I shall formulate the timelessness doctrine as the claim that God is *fundamentally* eternal, where the notion of fundamental eternality is different from the notion of that sort of eternality which involves the notion of unlimited duration.

OMNISCIENCE AND TIMELESSNESS

Is there a good reason to think that God is not fundamentally eternal? Some have claimed that there is a good reason, for they have thought that this doctrine is incompatible with the mutual affirmation of the doctrine of omniscience. The claim in question is that God cannot know propositions such as

(1) It is now 1 June 1984,

if He is fundamentally eternal. The argument, in summary, is as follows:

(2) If God is omniscient, God knows that it is now 1 June 1984.
(3) If God is fundamentally eternal, he cannot know that it is now 1 June 1984.
(4) God is omniscient.
(5) Therefore, God is in time.

The critical premise of this argument is (3). Premise (4) is uncontroversial, and premise (2) is true given the definition of omniscience presented in this work. Hence the issue is whether (3) is true or not.

What we wish to know is whether in order for God to know both

(1) It is now 1 June 1984

and

(6) It is now 2 June 1984

on successive days, He must be a temporal being. Must He know (1) at one time, and only come to know (6) later? Prior thinks the answer is yes:

> God could not, on the view I am considering, know that the 1960 final examinations at Manchester are now over. For this isn't something that he or anyone could know timelessly, because it isn't true timelessly. It's true now but it wasn't a year ago (I write this on 29 August 1960) and so far as I can see all that can be said on this subject timelessly is that the finishing date of the 1960 final examinations is an earlier one than the 29th August, and this is not the thing we know when we know that those examinations are over. I cannot think of any better way of showing this than one I've used before, namely the argument that what we know when we know that the 1960 final examinations are over can't be just a timeless relation between dates, because this isn't the thing we're pleased about when we're pleased the examinations are over.[3]

As I understand this argument, it proceeds as follows:

(7) The final examinations of 1960 are now over.

(8) If (7) can be known by a timeless being, then (7) must be the same as:

(9) The final examinations of 1960 are earlier than 29 August 1960.

(10) It is possible that a person is pleased that (7) is true, and not have a pleasant or unpleasant attitude towards (9).

(11) If (10), then (7) is not the same proposition as (9).

(12) Hence, (7) is not identical to (9).

(13) Therefore, a timeless or changeless being cannot know (7).

This argument is not convincing as it stands, for premise (8) is not obviously true. So why should one think that (8) is true? The answer, at least for Prior, is to be found in the connection between time and tense. Perhaps the worry is that, if a being knows anything involving tense, then that being must be in time. Thus if a being knows that Nixon used to be President, then that being is in time, located at some present moment later than the time at which Nixon was President. Or, again, if a person knows that Reagan will win the election, knowing that proposition implies a location in time earlier than the time at which Reagan wins the election.

Some have claimed that the only sort of knowledge a timeless being could have is the sort arrived at by replacing tensed knowledge with multi-tensed alternatives to that knowledge.[4] Instead of knowing that Nixon used to be President, a timeless being could only know that Nixon is, was, or will be President in 1972. Thus, in order to defend that God is both timeless and omniscient, one must find multi-tensed alternatives that are God's knowledge to the tensed knowledge that we have.

There is another alternative that might be proposed, which is that there is a tenseless sense of any verb which is not equivalent either to the present tense of that verb or to the multi-tense alternative. Examples of such a tenseless sense include instances of mathematical knowledge: when I claim that $2 + 2 = 4$, I am not claiming that $2 + 2$ is (now) 4 nor am I claiming that $2 + 2$ is, was, and always will be 4. What I say may imply these latter claims, but it is not identical to them. Hence, perhaps in a tenseless verb, we might be able to capture God's timeless knowledge.

In either case, it appears that the truth of (8) is being granted. (9) appears most like the tenseless alternative, though it could just as easily be that the verb in it is a place-holder for 'is, was, or will be'. In either case, it seems that we have the following argument that (8) is true:

(14) A proposition can be known by a timeless being if and only if that proposition is not an essentially temporal proposition.

(15) A proposition is an essentially temporal proposition if and only if it is not possible to express that proposition without implying temporal indexicals.

(16) A proposition is expressed without implying temporal indexicals if and only if the tense of the verb used in expressing that proposition is either tenseless or multi-tense.

(17) Therefore, if (7) is true, it must be identical to (9) or some other proposition like (9) expressible without implying temporal indexicals.

(18) There is no other candidate than (9) to be identical to (7) expressible without implying temporal indexicals.

(19) Therefore, if (7) is true, it must be identical to (9).

We then have an argument (in (2)–(5)) for the claim that God cannot be omniscient unless He is in time. We also have an argument (in (7)–(13)) for the critical premise (3) of the original argument; and we have a final argument (in (14)–(19)) for the critical premise (8) of the intermediate argument. Since this argument for an inconsistency between timelessness and omniscience rests on claims about the temporality of much of our discourse, i.e. our use of temporal terms such as 'now', 'today', 'then', 'yesterday', etc., let us begin our evaluation of it by considering more closely the nature of the propositions expressed by such temporal discourse.

I defended earlier that the content of an intentional attitude of believing or knowing is a proposition, hence the question that we must address concerns the nature of the propositions expressed by temporal discourse. Consider again the proposition that

(1) It is now 1 June 1984.

That proposition is true; tomorrow, in order to express a true proposition, I would have to assert the sentence

(21) 'It is now 2 June 1984.'

Note first that (21) is not identical to

(7) It is now 2 June 1984.

(7) is a proposition, and a false one; (21) is a sentence which, if used today, would express a false proposition. However, if used tomorrow to express (7), what (21) would express would be a true proposition.

The question we need to ask concerns the nature of propositions like (1) and (7). In particular, we need to know what the word 'now' expresses. In some views, the word 'now' refers to a substance which moves through time. Such views are quite implausible – the word 'now' is simply a demonstrative that picks out or refers to a certain moment of time (the present one), not some sort of thing that moves through time. Here I shall merely assume and not argue for the view that time is real, hence I am assuming that there are such things as moments of time. Given P1 from the last chapter (P1 claimed that everything has an essence), such moments have essences. So we can say that the demonstrative 'now' expresses the essence of the moment of time to which it refers. Therefore, proposition (1) above implies:

(1A) The essence of the moment picked out by the use of the demonstrative 'now' in (1) is mutually exemplified with the property of being 1 June 1984.

Our discussions so far would seem to lead us to a response to the argument for the incompatibility between omniscience and timelessness, given that temporal demonstratives are just particular ways of referring to the essences of moments. First, we might claim that because a certain proposition is expressed at present with a use of demonstrative such as 'now', it does not follow that the essence of the moment picked out by the use of that demonstrative is inaccessible to a timeless being. All that the use of the demonstrative shows is how we, as temporal beings, access the essence in question. Further to know temporal propositions such as (1) and (7) does not require being subject to some sort of temporal becoming if all there is to knowing (1) and (7) is being acquainted with the particular essences in question. God, from the standpoint of eternity, is acquainted with the essence of every moment of time; and thus, even though we are subject to temporal becoming, a becoming which is reflected in the way in which we move (through time) from knowing propositions like (1) to propositions like (7), there might seem to be no good reason to think that this particular way of accessing the essences in question is necessary. Hence, it might be argued, the apparent incompatibility between timelessness and omniscience disappears.

We can put this sort of response in perspective by noting which of the original premises this response denies. It denies premise (3) (that God cannot know that it is now a certain day if he is not in time); and the denial of (3) proceeds by denying the critical premise (8) of the argument for (3). (8) claimed that a certain sort of translation of apparently temporal knowledge must be accurate for a non-temporal being to have knowledge of the same claim. The way in which (8) is denied is by claiming that the apparent infection of propositions such as (1) by temporality is eliminated by noting that (1A) lacks this temporality and further contains all the same temporal elements as (1). If (1A) is not identical to (1), it is not because of some temporal dimension; it must be for some other reason. Hence, in the defence of premise (8), the false premise is either (17) or (18). It might be claimed that (1) has not been replaced by a proposition identical to it, even though it has been shown that the temporal dimensions of (1) do not require temporal becoming in order to have knowledge of it; or one might claim that in (1A) there has been given the start of a translation still to be completed in which the temporal content of (1) is neutralised. In any case, there is no good argument for (8), and (8) ought to be rejected, according to this response.

This response to the above argument does not end the discussion though, for there is another argument which bears on the relation between omniscience and timelessness. For one way to show that incompatibility still remains between timelessness and omniscience is to show that in being acquainted with the essences of moments, some sort of change must occur in any being who is omniscient from moment to moment. For if a being undergoes change, then it is true that such a being has a property at one time which is lacking at another time. Yet if a being comes to have a property which was lacking previously, then that being has an existence which involves duration from the first time to the second. Since our understanding of the fundamental eternality of God prohibits an involvement with the notion of duration, it follows that if God is not immutable, then He is not fundamentally eternal either. Let us turn, then, to the argument for the supposed incompatibility between immutability and omniscience.

OMNISCIENCE AND IMMUTABILITY

The argument calls for us to consider Hume and Heimsohn on two different days (1 June and 2 June) in 1760. On 1 June 1760, Hume believes the proposition expressed by the sentence 'it is now raining'. The question that I wish to consider is whether Heimsohn can believe, on 2 June, exactly what Hume believes on 1 June. It might be thought that it is very easy for him to believe the same thing; he need only believe the proposition expressed for him on 2 June by the sentence 'yesterday it was raining', 'it was then (yesterday) raining'.

The same objection arises to the claimed identity here that arose in Chapter 2 to the claimed identity between Hume believing what is expressed by 'I'm Hume' and Heimsohn believing 'he's Hume'; namely, that the behaviour that would result from such beliefs is quite different. But it might be claimed, if two persons are in identical total mental states, it is at least highly probable (if not entailed) that their behaviour (relevant to that state) is the same. In the case of the indexical 'now', believing what is expressed by that term generates quite different behaviour from what is generated by believing what is expressed by the term 'then'. Presuming they are both planning to be outdoors, it is probable that Hume would make some sort of provision for avoiding getting wet; it is not probable at all that Heimsohn would. Therefore, the mental state of Hume in believing that it is now raining must be significantly different from that of Heimsohn in believing that it was then raining in order to explain the difference in their behaviour.

This argument regarding the temporal indexicals 'now' and 'then' is not only an argument for the incompatibility between immutability and omniscience, it is also an argument which affects the theory of direct grasping presented in Chapter 2. For just as in the case of propositions expressed by the pronouns 'I' and 'he', the options are limited, if we grant the soundness of these arguments. One can opt for propositions with limited access; propositions which only the person in question can access, propositions which can only be accessed at a particular time, and propositions which can only be accessed at a particular place. I found earlier that such private, or accessibly limited, propositions were problematic when they were expressed by the word 'I'; this theory about accessibly limited propositions about times and places are equally problematic, for counter-examples to accessibly limited temporal propositions are as easy to construct as are counter-examples to private, personal propositions. If Liar Larry said yesterday, 'I am now the leader of my neighbourhood gang', I would not believe him. But, after checking it out in the meantime and discovering that Larry had just been elected leader moments before he told me, I might return to Larry and apologetically intone, 'I have now come to see that what you told me yesterday is true.' What this quasi-apology amounts to is an assertion that I have come to believe today what Larry asserted yesterday. But if the propositions including temporal elements are accessibly limited to the time with which they are concerned, I cannot strictly speaking be said to believe today what Larry asserted yesterday;

for what Larry asserted yesterday could only be the object of any intentional attitude yesterday. Yet clearly, I can believe what Larry asserted yesterday; hence the proposition which he asserted cannot be accessibly limited to the time which it is about. So we have as much reason to reject limitations of access regarding time as we did regarding personal essences.

What is true about such cases is that the meanings of the sentences used to express the proposition in question are different. So, for example, the sentences 'it is now raining' and 'it was then raining' have different meanings, but we have already noted that the proposition expressed by a sentence ought not be confused with the meaning of that sentence; we should not infer that there are different propositions which are the objects of belief when one person (today) believes what is expressed for him by 'it is now raining', and another person (tomorrow) believes what is expressed for him by 'it was then raining'. In accordance with the triadic theory of belief defended in Chapter 2, what can be said is that the same propositional object is *accessed* through different sentences with different meanings.

Our earlier distinction between direct grasping and indirect grasping can be used here as well, but the principles governing these notions need to be altered. We had said in Chapter 2 that if one grasps a proposition directly, then that proposition was about oneself. We should also allow, it would seem, that one can grasp directly propositions about the spatially and temporally present as well. Thus we need to replace P4 with:

P4': For all x and y, if x grasps y directly, then either (i) y includes x's essence, (ii) y includes the essence of the place where x is, or (iii) y includes the essence of the moment which is identical to the essence of the moment at which x directly grasps y.

And P6 gives way to:

P6': For all x, y, and z, if x grasps y directly, then y is necessarily such that, for all z such that z is non-identical to x and does not share the same present place or moment with x, z does not directly grasp y.

We grasp the present directly (moment or place) and only indirectly grasp other moments or places because, if questioned sufficiently, we determinately fix reference to any other time or place with reference to the present place or moment. We seem sometimes to be able to specify times in terms of a certain calendar, as when we say the American

Revolution began in 1776; but if pushed concerning that calendar, we must in the end identify its dating procedures in terms of the present moment. Hence there is a certain sort of intimacy with the present moment or place which we do not share with any other moment or place.

TIMELESSNESS, IMMUTABILITY AND OMNIPRESENCE

The argument for the incompatibility of immutability and omniscience thus forces us to a deeper understanding of the distinction between direct and indirect grasping. Given this understanding, can we defend the compatibility between immutability (and hence timelessness) and omniscience?

The principles above open up several possibilities which we need to explore. One possibility for defending the consistency of these doctrines would be to affirm that God does not directly grasp any temporal moment. In accord with the above principles, if God does not directly grasp any proposition including temporal aspects, it does not follow that He is not omniscient. For even if He only indirectly grasps all temporal moments, it is still the case that He can know all true propositions. Hence it might be thought that one can affirm the doctrines of timelessness, immutability and omniscience by affirming that God indirectly grasps every temporal moment, and directly grasps none of them.

One might think that the following objection could be given to this view. Since God is maximally, in particular, cognitively perfect, He could not be cognitively perfect without directly grasping some moments of time. Just as we cannot hold the view that God is never intimately enough acquainted with himself to know himself as himself, so it would be a mark of imperfection were God never to be intimately acquainted with any temporal or spatial location.

If this objection is correct, there are still two other options left open. First, both the timelessness doctrine and the immutability doctrines might be rejected. One might argue for this option as follows: if God does directly grasp some moments and not others in a way that exhibits maximal perfection, it better be the *present* moment that He grasps directly. But if God is continually grasping the present moment directly, then He is going to have a property at one time that He lacked at an earlier one. Hence He would not be immutable in the strict sense and would not be timeless either.

But there is another option. One might attempt to defend the consistency of the three doctrines by affirming that God not only grasps some temporal moments directly, He grasps them all directly. Such a view implies that, for God, all temporal moments are immediately and directly experienced by Him so that He is not subject to any of the remoteness which we experience concerning the past and future.

One reason for affirming this view is that it is analogous with a plausible construal of omnipresence. That construal is:

OP: Being *B* is omnipresent = $_{df.}$ *B* grasps directly the essence of every spatial location.

Affirming that God grasps all temporal moments directly would then be the temporal analogue of holding that all places are "here" for God, i.e. since every place is "here" for God, so is every time "now" for God. Both 'here' and 'now' express the essences of the moments or places in question, and if being omnipresent is to be construed by OP, it might be thought that God should also be acquainted with movements of time in a direct way as well. So perhaps God grasps all moments of time.

It might be thought that there is the following objection to this view. As I asserted in Chapter 2, the distinction between direct and indirect grasping is to be explained by a triadic theory of belief in which there is a relation between an intentional attitude, a proposition, and a meaning. But to believe a proposition through the meaning of 'it is now Tuesday' is different from believing that same proposition through the meaning of 'it was then (yesterday) Tuesday'. Yet if God is to grasp the proposition in question directly both today and tomorrow, what constant meaning could there be by virtue of which He accesses that proposition?

The answer to this question is simple once it is noted that words like 'now' and 'then' are demonstratives which refer to moments of time. As noted already, for temporal creatures such as ourselves, the meaning of the first allows us to access the proposition in question in a more direct fashion than the meaning of the second. What is needed, then, for an atemporal being is some device for referring to moments of time that is equally direct at any moment of time. Such a device would be a name for each moment of time, and if demonstratives are substantially referential in meaning, then the names would have to be so as well. The solution to the puzzle of the last paragraph is not very difficult; God need only have a name for each moment of time.

We should note, however, that if this view is acceptable, an atemporal being rarely has literally the same beliefs as temporal beings. For the proposition in question, though the same for each, will rarely be accessed through the same meaning; at least not with regard to propositions which, for a temporal being, are about the past. Though this is an implication of the above account, it does not seem to present any problem which I can see.

There is a stronger objection to this view because, given P6′, if God grasps a proposition directly involving time, then the moment of time in question is present for God. Yet some have claimed that this puts God in the ridiculous position of experiencing everything as happening simultaneously. Kenny, for example, claims:

> The whole concept of a timeless eternity, the whole of which is simultaneous with every part of time, seems to be radically incoherent. For simultaneity as ordinarily understood is a transitive relation. If A happens at the same time as B, and B happens at the same time as C, then A happens at the same time as C. If the BBC programme and the ITV programme both start when the Big Ben strikes ten, then they both start at the same time. But, on St. Thomas' view, my typing of this paper is simultaneous with the whole of eternity. Again, on this view, the great fire of Rome is simultaneous with the whole of eternity. Therefore, while I type these words, Nero fiddles heartlessly on.[5]

Kenny discusses this only as an objection to Aquinas' view, but it would seem to be equally applicable to the view defended above whereon God grasps every temporal moment directly. Further, if the above theory has the implications Kenny claims regarding Aquinas' view, then it is inadequate for as a result, God would be quite confused about what was happening when.

The objection is not decisive, however, for the apparent incoherence here can be avoided in two ways. First, we might take a cue from the treatment of the notion of simultaneity in relativity theory in order to resolve the matter. For we have learned (or should have learned) to exhibit a great deal of care in employing our ordinary notion of simultaneity, given the development of relativity theory. In this theory, there is no such thing as simultaneity *simpliciter*, there is only simultaneity *within a frame of reference*. Just so, perhaps we should distinguish what is simultaneous *from the standpoint of eternity* from what is sumultaneous *from some temporal standpoint*. If we distinguish these two notions, and claim that neither is reducible to the other, we can no longer infer that God is confused about the course of history if He is timeless. The proper claim would be that, from the standpoint of eternity, God knows as (eternally) present every event which, from some temporal standpoint, has occurred, is occurring, or will occur.[6]

The other way to escape this difficulty is to alter P6′ so that it does not require that any moment be a present moment in order to be grasped directly. One might, for example, attempt to restrict the application of P6′ to non-omniscient beings, while allowing that omniscient beings can grasp essences of moments directly without being in time.

Such a restriction needs some sort of defence, though, for one should not simply assert that a general principle applies to all beings except one without some explanation as to why that being is exempt from the principle in question. What we need is a specification of some property an omniscient being has or might have which would imply that such a being could grasp moments directly without being in time. The most plausible property would be that of being omnipotent. One might say, for example, that being omnipotent distinguishes a being from all other possible beings with regard to the abilities one has, so that being omnipotent implies that one can grasp directly what no other (temporally bound) person can.

How plausible this final response is, is questionable; but at least the first response distinguishing frames of temporal reference is quite plausible. There is thus good reason for dismissing Kenny's objection to both Aquinas' view and this one.

TIMELESS KNOWLEDGE AND TIMELESS ACTION

We have seen how to defend the compatibility of the doctrines of timelessness, immutability, and omniscience. However, in order for the doctrine of immutability to be retained, some explanation is called for concerning how an immutable being can participate in the history of human affairs without being subject to change. If God acts in history, there is some need to explain how this can be done by a timeless and immutable being. Seeing what must be claimed here will help in understanding how it might be possible for a timeless and immutable being to grasp every temporal moment directly even though not every temporal moment is present (for us).

In order to defend the doctrine of immutability, we will need an account of the notion of an *eternal action*. The necessity of this supplement arises from noting that, if God acts in history (as I shall assume He does), it would appear initially that in order to understand how He picks one particular moment in which to act, He must distinguish that moment from all others in some way. A natural response here is to suggest that He distinguishes the moments in question by considering when He wishes to intervene and then doing so when that moment becomes present. If God bears the same grasping relation (direct or indirect) to all temporal moments, it would appear that there is no distinction for Him between those which allow such recognition. In addition, if He at one time recognises some moment and at another recognises a different moment as present, then He is not, strictly speaking, immutable.

In order to handle this problem, we must, as indicated above, claim that God's actions are all *eternal actions*. Thus instead of saying that in 7 BC God had not yet sent His Son, but that by 7 AD He had, we should say that God performed the following actions (or omissions) eternally: not sending His son in 7 BC, and sending His Son at some time earlier than 7 AD.

In order to understand the notion of an eternal action, we first need a distinction between that aspect of an action which is internal to the agent and that which consists of some effect produced by that agent. The effects of our actions often occur at times other than when the original act was performed; for example, Jim might try to kill Joe by shooting him on Tuesday, though Joe does not actually die until Friday. This distinction allows an explanation of an eternal action; consider, for example, Alston's lucid account:

> The crucial point is that the two aspects can differ in temporal status. The worldly effect (of God's actions) will be at a time. But that is quite compatible with this that the divine volition should be timeless, should be embraced with all other divine activity in the one eternal *now*. The action is in time by virtue of its effect, but not by virtue of the immediate activity of the agent ... [So, h]ow can a timeless being act in the temporal world? By timelessly performing acts of will that have temporal effects.[7]

So the notion of an eternal action is one in which that aspect internal to the agent is timeless and the effect of which is in time; God acts in history by 'timelessly performing acts of will that have temporal effects'.

The distinction which allows an explanation of an eternal action also helps us to explain the direct grasping of every temporal moment by a timeless being. When knowledge occurs, there is a distinction between what is known and the knowing, just as there was a distinction above between the internal aspect of an action and the effects of that action. When a timeless being knows a fact infected with temporality, what is known is certainly temporal. However, the knowing of that fact can none the less itself be timeless. Further, if this distinction allows some sense to be made of a timeless being knowing what time it is, I see no principle reason for thinking that a timeless being cannot grasp the essence of every temporal moment directly, regardless of whether that moment is present for us or not. We might explain this claim by saying that God grasps directly whatever is "now" in the eternal *now*, even though what is present from the standpoint of eternity may be past or future from our own temporal standpoint.

CONCLUSION

Perhaps we can now see a limited defence of the doctrine of the compatibility of timelessness, omniscience, and immutability. I say a 'limited defence', for the above discussion falls rather short of a full explanation of the compatability claim precisely because it does not contain a full investigation of the doctrines of timelessness or immutability.

There is an even stronger sense in which this chapter only constitutes a limited defence of the compatibility of the three doctrines. Central to this defence is the notion of an eternal action, which must be coherent, or God cannot be immutable and yet act in history. Further, as we have seen, if God is not immutable in the strict sense under discussion here, He cannot be fundamentally eternal either.

This dependence on the concept of an eternal action makes our discussion tenuous at best, for even if it is possible to perform an act of will at t which has an effect at t', where t' is later than t, more than this possibility is required for God's willing, from eternity, to have temporal effects. In particular, it must be possible for a fundamentally eternal being causally to affect the temporal order; and this causal requirement is independent of the possibility of willing occurring in a different temporal framework from the effects of that willing. I do not know how to defend the possibility of the causal requirement; it would seem that we need to know quite a bit more about the nature of causality before such an investigation can be completed.

In conclusion, it is important to remind ourselves of the importance of the discussion for this work on omniscience. Originally, the doctrine of timelessness seemed necessary (to some) to avoid the problem of foreknowledge and freedom. Since we have seen that there really is no problem concerning foreknowledge and freedom anyway, we do not have the same reason to affirm the timelessness doctrine. Further, the strict immutability doctrine under consideration here is perhaps not central to any adequate conception of God. A less strict version of the doctrine, wherein it is affirmed that God's intentions and character are not subject to change, may still be adequate, even though we give up the view that God strictly undergoes no alteration whatsoever.

So even if the notion of an action from all eternity turns out to be incoherent, or if there are irresolvable problems with asserting that God grasps all temporal moments in the same way, it is only the doctrines of timelessness and (classical) immutability that face problems; the doctrine of omniscience is logically independent of these. My intention has been only to show that it is not quite as simple as has been thought to show that God could not be timeless or strictly immutable, and, further, that it is not obvious that coherent versions of those doctrines are incompatible with the doctrine of omniscience.

My inclination is to think that the timelessness of God should be defended, if it is to be defended, by claiming that God grasps every temporal moment directly. There is some positive ground for this view on the basis of the analogy between God's knowledge of spatial location and His knowledge of temporal location. This analogy is based on the analogous nature of the demonstratives 'here' and 'now'. However, these considerations are not decisive; and I certainly do not mean to suggest that if this version of the timelessness doctrine is to be rejected that we must give up omnipresence as well. The omnipresence doctrine might be retained as it is, or it might also be construed as a property which obtains in virtue of God's knowledge of and/or power over all spatial regions.

In conclusion, we can say that, regardless of whether the suggestions of this chapter are able to withstand more thorough investigation, the doctrine of omniscience presented earlier is in no difficulty. Whereas the classical doctrines of timelessness and immutability have little support, the doctrine of omniscience is a firmly established doctrine. Thus if any incompatibility should be present, that problem is one for the classical doctrines of immutability and timelessness, not for the doctrine of omniscience.

6 Conclusion

Historically, the important issues surrounding the doctrine of omniscience have been the problem of the compatibility between God's foreknowledge and human freedom, and the implication of any solution to that problem. For many, the solution to the foreknowledge issue has been to hold that God is a timeless being: that, for Him, there is no distinction between past, present, and future as there is for us; and so, strictly speaking, God has no *fore*knowledge at all.

Of course, there were additional motivations for maintaining the timelessness doctrine besides the fact that it provides a neat solution to the freedom–foreknowledge problem. Given the Aristotelian understanding of time as the measure of change, it is plausible to think that time is created by God in conjunction with His creation of the rest of the universe in which change occurs. Another motivation is the desire to distinguish God's everlastingness from the everlastingness of changeable, alterable things. Again, the Aristotelian view that the world has always been may provide motivation here for the timelessness doctrine, for surely Christians and other theists did not wish to hold that God is everlasting in the same way that the universe might have been thought to be.

These motivations, though, do not imply the timelessness doctrine. The Aristotelian view of time is more appropriately a view about what grounds our measurement of time than a view about time itself. Further, the problematic dimension of changeable substances is their corruptibility, not the mere fact that they change in some respect or other; hence if change is compatible with continued perfection (as it seems to be), then the fact that God is everlasting and yet changeable does not prevent a distinction between His everlastingness and the everlastingness of other things. He is incorruptible, they are not. Thus, if there is an argument for the timelessness doctrine, it is not to be found in the traditional motivations for that doctrine.

Whatever the motivations for affirming a timelessness doctrine, it seemed to many that the doctrine of omniscience was rescued by positing another doctrine (the timelessness doctrine) even more obviously incoherent than the original doctrine of omniscience. So the discussions of omniscience have tended to centre around the relationship between and coherence of the doctrines of omniscience, timelessness and immutability, as well as on the relationship between omniscience and human freedom. This work covers these topics as well, for I have tried to show how these various topics are related; however, I have also defended that the acceptability of the doctrine of omniscience is independent of the acceptability of these other doctrines. The motivations for the doctrines of timelessness and immutability fall far short of requiring those doctrines; the motivations for the doctrine of omniscience are much stronger. Thus even if the doctrines of timelessness and immutability are problematic, it does not follow that the doctrine of omniscience faces any serious difficulty.

The heart of the theory of omniscience that I have developed may be called a Molinist account of omniscience. This part of the theory explains how God knows the future without its being necessitated in any fashion whatsoever. The intuitive idea of the theory is that there are true statements about what a person would freely do, were he in certain circumstances. If one leaves a child in the kitchen in clear view of a full and reachable biscuit tin, what that child will do is obvious: he is going to eat a biscuit (or two). For each of us, there is a maximal conjunction of claims of this sort that correctly state what each of us would do in certain circumstances. God knows the future, and knew what He was doing at creation by virtue of knowing these maximal subjunctives of freedom.

How does God know these maximal subjunctives of freedom? In the standard semantics for such subjunctives, any subjunctive is true because of similarity relations between various possible worlds and the actual world. Such a theory may be adequate regarding subjunctives of freedom as well. First, this theory should not be rejected because there is no actual world before God creates. That objection is based on a confusion about the notion of the actual world. Since it is impossible that there be no actual world, it is impossible for there not to have been an actual world before creation. A more serious objection, though, centres on the possibility of two worlds sharing exactly the same history and yet being such that in one, a person acts in one way, and in the other, he/she acts another. The difficulty is in determining which of these worlds is most similar to the actual world. I have suggested that there is only one way for the standard semantics to solve this problem, and that is to hold that individuals have basic natures which explain the truth of the subjunctives of freedom in question.

On the other hand, should this response fail, we should not conclude that the Molinist view presented here faces any difficulty. Rather, it is the standard semantics that are in jeopardy, for the semantics are to be developed to account for what are intuitive truths. A completely unacceptable view of theory construction allows one to develop a theory and jettison intuitive truths because they do not fit the theory that has been developed.

The Molinist account of God's foreknowledge provides an explanation of how God know what will be done freely. Such an account supports the approach I defended to solving the logical puzzle concerning the relationship between foreknowledge and freedom. I asserted that there was no incompatibility between the two unless God could not be essentially omniscient. Since the Molinist account explains both how God knows the future free actions of humans and how God can have this sort of knowledge essentially, it follows that there is no incompatibility between foreknowledge and freedom.

The tasks described so far are rather traditional ones for any plausible defence of the doctrine of omniscience. In recent years, the need for further discussion has become apparent in light of contemporary theories concerning our awareness of ourselves and others. There has always been the need for work in basic epistemology in order to understand the doctrines of omniscience, and centuries of exploration have led to what I have called the traditional construal of omniscience. With regard to those issues, this work has mostly been silent; for it has not been my purpose to discuss issues in basic epistemology except in so far as they indicate problems for the doctrine of omniscience. Thus, for example, whether knowledge and belief are of different kinds or not does not seem to create any special problems for the doctrine of omniscience; nor, for most of the history of philosophy, has it seemed problematic that a reductive account of the objects of knowledge was to be favoured. Most recent epistemologists have held a propositional theory; though this view by no means exhausts the historical alternatives (for example, one might hold that knowledge is knowledge of essences rather than propositions). However, the import of the contemporary theories of self- and other-awareness is quite different, for if these theories are true, the doctrine of omniscience itself faces difficulties. First, a unified account of the objects of knowledge may have to be jettisoned; but worse, the very possibility of omniscience may be in jeopardy. These problems cast doubt on a whole way of thinking about omniscience, and thus have a more immediate and telling impact on discussions of that doctrine than do other issues in basic epistemology. It is for these reasons that a thorough investigation of these topics is included here, while other important issues in basic epistemology have been ignored.

Thus a large portion of this discussion of the doctrine of omniscience centred around the problems for the traditional account of omniscience, in which a being is omniscient just in case that being knows all truths. Since it is propositions which are either true or false, this traditional account supposes that a being can be omniscient by knowing all true propositions. In recent discussion, the reductionist view of the objects of intentional attitudes that lies behind this account has been challenged, most strongly by issues surrounding what has been called *de re* and *de se* awareness. Some have suggested that these sorts of awareness suggest that a different kind of reductive account ought to be accepted, one in which the object of intentional attitudes is a property, not a proposition. Others have suggested that the propositional account can still be defended if it is supplemented with additional features which imply that some propositions are private propositions: they are propositions which only some persons, at only some times and only some places, can access.

I have maintained that neither of these alternatives is acceptable. First, the property theory has the difficulty that it cannot properly explain what it is to conceive of one's own non-existence. That theory inevitably interprets such a conception as something impossible, for it must claim that one is conceiving oneself to have a property which implies one's own non-existence. It is impossible to have a property of that sort, yet it is not impossible that one does not exist. Hence the property theory is inadequate.

Further, one ought not to accept any view which posits the existence of private propositions, for you can believe what I believe about myself, you can believe tomorrow what I believe today, and you can believe where you are what I believe about where I am. Perhaps this identity of beliefs here is only a loose identity so that strictly speaking you cannot believe what I believe. However, one must have very strong reasons for denying the strict identity here, for it is intuitively obvious that there is such an identity; hence one ought not to accept the doctrine of private propositions unless one is forced to.

I have also argued that there are theological motivations for rejecting the possibility of private propositions. God knows us better than we know ourselves, yet if there are private propositions there is a sense in which we know ourselves best of all. Thus there are both theological and philosophical motivations for rejecting the possibility of private, or accessibly limited propositions.

Further, we have seen how to avoid such propositions through the distinction between direct and indirect grasping. In particular, this distinction involves the rejection of a dyadic theory of belief in favour of a triadic theory of belief. I have also suggested that what grounds the distinction between directly and indirectly grasped propositions is the meaning of the sentence used to express the proposition in question. The meanings of some terms, I have suggested, tie us in a more intimate fashion to certain features of the world; in particular, to ourselves, the present moment, and the present place. This distinction between direct and indirect grasping has its grounding in our intuitions that we bear a special relation to ourselves which we bear to nothing else; that we are more intimately associated with what is here and now than to what was then or what is or was there. The proposition expressed by the sentence 'I am here now' is one to which we have an especially intimate and immediate connection. The way in which the present theory of omniscience captures this connection is by claiming that this proposition and others like it are ones that we grasp directly by virtue of being expressed by sentences which refer in an especially immediate way to oneself, the present moment, and the present place.

When sentences such as this are used to pick out individuals other than ourselves, times other than the present, and spaces other than the local, such propositions are more remote and distant to our conceptual apparatus – we can only grasp such propositions indirectly. Yet two qualifications are necessary. First, though I think it is impossible for anyone other than oneself to grasp a proposition directly about oneself, it is not clear that it is impossible for a person to grasp directly places other than the local for me and times other than the present for me. The spatial point is obvious: clearly, people in Russia grasp directly those propositions which include the essence of some part of Russia, and I do not. The temporal point is also quite obvious when it is noted that yesterday I grasped the essence of a time directly which is not now the present.

A less obvious point may also hold about both locations and moments. It may be possible for a being to grasp directly the essence of every location, thereby being omnipresent. And, further, an individual may be able to grasp directly the essence of every moment – at least I do not see any good argument that this is impossible. If this direct grasping is possible, then a somewhat surprising result emerges from the consideration of indexicals. Whereas indexicals seemed, on the whole, to cast doubts on some of the traditional doctrines and/or formulations of the doctrines of immutability and timelessness, here we find a strong defence of both doctrines against the attacks brought by considerations regarding indexicals. If it is possible for a being to grasp directly all temporal moments at once just as it seems possible for a person to grasp directly all spatial locations at once, then there may be some sense to be made of the notion of God's being outside time. Thus whereas investigation of indexicals has led most recent philosophers to reject the timelessness doctrine, perhaps that rejection was rather premature.

The conclusion to be drawn from this discussion can be summed up as follows. A Molinistic account of omniscience and essential omniscience, combined with a traditional construal of omniscience as knowledge of all truths, is adequate. Such an account implies that an omniscient being knows everything there is to know without requiring that such a being be causally responsible for the actions of persons. Hence such an account does not imply that human beings are not free.

One final qualification is necessary about this conclusion. To say that a being is omniscient is not to say that such a being exhibits maximal cognitive perfection. Since no being could be God without being maximally perfect with regard to cognition, we ought also to affirm that God exhibits cognitive perfections other than omniscience. God not only knows all truths, He is intimately aware of His own nature and is as intimately acquainted with the natures of every other thing in the universe as He can be. These properties are also possessed essentially by God: no matter how the world might have turned out, God would have been maximally cognitively perfect.

Notes and References

1 The Range of Knowledge

1. Peter Geach, *Providence and Evil* (Cambridge: Cambridge University Press) chapter 3 'Omniscience and the Future'.
2. Ibid., pp. 52–3.
3. Ibid., p. 50.
4. Ibid., p. 52.
5. Ibid.
6. Richard Swinburne, *The Coherence of Theism* (Oxford: Oxford University Press, 1977) pp. 174–5.
7. Ibid., pp. 170–1.
8. Ibid., p. 175.
9. Here I ignore the need for a fourth condition in addition to justified true belief to account for Gettier-type counter-examples to the traditional construal of knowledge as justified true belief. In a later chapter, I will argue that in God's case, no such counter-examples can arise to the traditional construal; hence there is warrant for ignoring the fourth condition here. For recent discussion of Gettier's original counter-examples to the justified, true belief account of knowledge, and the literature generated by his paper, see Pappas and Swain (eds) *Essays on Knowledge and Justification* (Ithaca: Cornell University Press, 1978); and Robert Shope, *The Analysis of Knowing* (Princeton: Princeton University Press, 1983).
10. Swinburne, *The Coherence of Theism*, pp. 171–2.
11. Ibid.
12. Ibid., pp. 145–8. I do not mean to endorse Swinburne's view about the way in which a perfectly free being would act: I think there are serious problems with the view, but they do not affect this discussion. For it is at least true that God, since He is essentially good and rational, does whatever He has an overriding reason to do; and perhaps God is the only perfectly free agent there is.

2 Knowledge and Its Objects

1. Peter Geach, *Providence and Evil* (Cambridge: Cambridge University Press, 1977) p. 40.
2. Cf. David Armstrong, *Belief, Truth and Knowledge* (Cambridge: Cambridge University Press, 1973).
3. Cf. Alvin Goldman, 'What Is Justified Belief?', in George Pappas (ed.)

Justification and Knowledge (Dordrecht: D. Reidel, 1979) pp. 1–25; Fred Dretske, *Knowledge and the Flow of Information* (Boston: MIT Press, 1981).

4. Edmund Gettier, 'Is Justified True Belief Knowledge?', *Analysis*, 23 (1963) pp. 121–3.

5. Patrick Grim, 'Some Neglected Problems of Omniscience', *American Philosophical Quarterly*, 20 (1983) p. 266. I have taken the liberty of substituting the name 'O' for the account of omniscience in question where Grim originally had 'Df. 3'.

6. Willard Van Orman Quine, 'Quantifiers and Propositional Attitudes', in his *The Ways of Paradox* (New York: Random House, 1966) pp. 185–96.

7. Bertrand Russell, 'The Philosophy of Logical Atomism', in R. C. Marsh (ed.) *Logic and Knowledge* (New York: Capricorn Books, 1956) pp. 175–282.

8. Bertrand Russell, 'On the Nature of Acquaintance', in *Logic and Knowledge*, p.130.

9. David Kaplan, 'Quantifying In', in D. Davidson and J. Hintikka (eds) *Words and Objections* (Dordrecht: D. Reidel, 1969) pp. 206–42.

10. Ernest Sosa, 'Propositional Attitudes De Dicto and De Re', *The Journal of Philosophy*, 67, (1970) pp. 883–96.

11. Ibid., p. 892.

12. Roderick Chisholm, *Person and Object* (La Salle: Open Court, 1976) Appendix C.

13. Ibid., p. 169.

14. Ibid.

15. Ibid.

16. Ibid.

17. Tyler Burge, 'Belief De Re', *The Journal of Philosophy*, 74 (1977) pp. 338–61.

18. Myles Brand, 'Intending and Believing', in James Tomberlin (ed.) *Agent, Language, and the Structure of the World* (Indianapolis: Hackett, 1983) pp. 181–2.

19. John Perry, 'The Problem of the Essential Indexical', *Nous*,13 (1979) p. 3.

20. Ibid., pp. 4–5.

21. Chisholm defends this view in *Person and Object*.

22. Ibid., pp. 33–6.

23. Ibid.

24. Ibid.

25. G. E. M. Anscombe, 'The First Person', in Samuel Guttenplan (ed.) *Mind and Language* (Oxford: Oxford University Press, 1975) p. 61.

26. 'The First Person', p. 21.

27. Hector Castaneda, *Thinking and Doing* (Dordrecht: D. Reidel, 1975) p. 159.

28. 'On the Phenomeno-Logic of the I', *Akten des XIV. Internationalen Kongresses fur Philosphie*, III (Vienna: University of Vienna, 1969) pp. 260–9.

29. Ernest Sosa, 'Consciousness of the Self and of the Present', in Tomberlin (ed.) *Agent, Language, and the Structure of the World*, p. 140.

30. Sosa, p. 141.
31. Cf. Roderick Chisholm, *The First Person*; John Perry, 'The Problem of the Essential Indexical'; David Lewis, 'Attitudes de dicto and de se', *The Philosophical Review*, 88, (1979) pp. 513–43.
32. Anscombe, 'The First Person', p. 24.
33. Ibid., p. 28.
34. Ibid.
35. Ibid., p. 31.
36. Ibid.
37. Peter J. Markie develops this criticism of Chisholm's property theory in detail in 'De Dicto and De Se', *Philosophical Studies*, 45, (1984) pp. 231–8.
38. Chisholm most clearly affirms this view in correspondence with Peter J. Markie on issues surrounding Markie's criticism of Chisholm's property view.
39. This definition is one suggested to me by Edward Wierenga in correspondence.
40. I owe awareness of both the arguments to discussions with Peter J. Markie.
41. Chisholm suggests this view in *Person and Object*, pp. 31–7.
42. For a discussion and bibliography concerning the issues surrounding a triadic theory of belief which takes the meaning of the sentence to be one component of belief, cf. Mark Richard, 'Direct Reference and Ascriptions of Belief', *Journal of Philosophical Logic* 12, (1983) pp. 425–52.
43. Reliabilist theories of justification are especially guilty of confusing epistemic ideality with justification. They claim that a justified belief is a belief produced by a reliable mechanism. Yet, what mechanisms are reliable is sometimes a matter of what epistemic dispositions a person has to form beliefs, and thus reliabilists claim that unless a person has proper dispositions to form beliefs, many of his beliefs will be unjustified. This seems to me to confuse what we want an epistemically ideal agent to be like (we want him not only to justifiably believe all and only what is true, but to be disposed to form beliefs conforming to this requirement as well) with whether a person has a justified belief at present. Justified beliefs can be obtained in the process of forming our intellectual characters (even in the midst of, and as a result of, intellectual deficiencies) just as morally proper behaviour can occur even in the morally tainted.

    For more discussion on this matter, see Keith Lehrer's gypsy lawyer example in *Knowledge*, pp. 124–5 (Oxford: Oxford University Press, 1974), and my own 'How to Be a Reliabilist', forthcoming, *American Philosophical Quarterly*, 1986.

3 God's Certainty and Man's Freedom

1. See, for example, Boethius, *The Consolation of Philosophy*, Book V; Augustine, *De Libero Arbitrio*, Bk. III; Leibniz, *Theodicee*, Part I.

2. Augustine, *De Libero Arbitrio*, Book III, translated by J. H. S. Burleigh, *Augustine's Earlier Writings* (Philadelphia: Fortress Press, 1955).

3. Fredreich Schleiermacher, *The Christian Faith*, Part I, Section 2, paragraph 55, translated by W. R. Matthew (Edinburgh: Clark (T and T), 1928) p. 228.

4. Augustine, *De Libero Arbitrio*.

5. David Hume, *An Enquiry Concerning Human Understanding*, Section VII (New York: Bobbs-Merrill, 1955).

6. Note Hume's actual words: 'we may define a cause to be an object followed by another, and where all the objects, similar to the first are objects similar to the second'.

7. This problem is just the problem logical positivists faced in attempting to separate law-like generalisations from mere regularities. Cf., e.g., A. J. Ayer, 'What is a Law of Nature?' and R. B. Braithwaite 'Laws of Nature and Causality', both in Baruch Brody (ed.) *Readings in the Philosophy of Science* (Englewood Cliffs: Prentice-Hall, 1970).

8. Sosa claims in his introduction to *Causation and Conditionals* (Oxford: Oxford University Press, 1975) that this is roughly the view defended by J. S. Mill (*Systems of Logic*, Book III, chapter V); R. B. Braithwaite (*Scientific Explanation*, pp. 315–18); H. L. A. Hart and A. M. Honore (*Causation in the Law*, Part I, pp. 106–7); C. G. Hempel (*Aspects of Scientific Explanation*, p. 349); and K. Popper (*Objective Knowledge*, p. 91).

9. Robert Stalnaker, 'A Theory of Conditionals', pp. 165–79 in Sosa, *Causation and Conditionals*; David Lewis, *Counterfactuals* (Oxford: Basil Blackwell, 1973).

10. Cf. Hume, *Enquiry*.

11. David Lewis, 'Causation', in Sosa, p. 187.

12. Ibid., pp. 186–7.

13. I borrow this counter-example from J. Kim, 'Causes and Counterfactuals', in Sosa, p. 193.

14. Lewis, 'Causation'; *Counterfactuals*; and 'Counterfactual Dependence and Time's Arrow', *Nous*, 13 (1979) pp. 455–76.

15. Marshall Swain, *Reasons and Knowledge* (Ithaca: Cornell University Press, 1981) pp. 58–65.

16. Boethius, *The Consolation of Philosophy* (New York: Bobbs-Merrill, 1962) pp 104–5.

17. Ibid., p. 105.

18. Richard Taylor, *Metaphysics*, 2nd edn (Englewood Cliffs: Prentice-Hall, 1978) pp. 66–7.

19. Thomas Aquinas, *Summa Theologica*, Part I, Question 14 in *Basic Writings of Saint Thomas Aquinas*, edited by Anton Pegis (New York: Random House, 1945).

20. Nelson Pike, 'Divine Omniscience and Voluntary Action', in Stephen Cahn and David Shatz (eds) *Contemporary Philosophy of Religion* (New York: Oxford University Press, 1982) pp. 61–76.

21. Ibid., p. 65.

22. Ibid.

23. Ibid., p. 66.

24. Alvin Plantinga, *God, Freedom and Evil* (New York: Harper Torchbooks, 1974).
25. Ibid., p. 71.
26. Ibid., p. 70.
27. Nelson Pike, 'Divine Foreknowledge, Human Freedom, and Possible Worlds', *Philosophical Review*, 86 (April, 1977) pp. 209–16.
28. Ibid., pp. 214, 215–6.
29. 'On Ockham's Way Out', *Faith and Philosophy*, forthcoming 1986.
30. Ibid. (p. 32 in typescript).
31. Ibid.
32. Ibid. (p. 31 in typescript).
33. For a defence of this requirement, cf. Thomas P. Flint and Alfred J. Freddoso, 'Maximal Power', in Alfred J. Freddoso (ed.) *The Existence & Nature of God* (Notre Dame: University of Notre Dame Press, 1983) pp. 81–114.
34. Marilyn Adams, 'Is the Existence of God a "Hard" Fact?' *Philosophical Review*, 76 (1967) pp. 493–4.
35. Ibid.
36. These problems for Adams's account are discussed in John Martin Fischer, 'Freedom and Foreknowledge', *Philosophical Review*, 92 (1983) pp. 67–79.
37. Fischer, p. 74.
38. Ibid., p. 75.
39. In the account of accidental necessity which I present here, I am greatly indebted to papers by Alfred Freddoso, 'Accidental Necessity and Logical Determinism', *The Journal of Philosophy*, 80 (1983) pp. 257–8, and 'Accidental Necessity and Power Over the Past', *Pacific Philosophical Quarterly*, 63 (1982) pp. 59–60; and to Joshua Hoffman and Gary Rosencrantz, 'Hard and Soft Facts', *The Philosophical Review*, 93, (1984) pp. 419–34. Their accounts allow either that propositions can vary in truth-value (Freddoso's account) or that states of affairs can obtain at some times and not at others (Hoffman-Rosencrantz). Since I prefer to avoid these views, the formulation I give is not identical to either of theirs.
40. I owe awareness of this issue to Thomas V. Morris. Further, the notion of an immemorial proposition I employ is a close cousin of Morris's notion of an immemorial property in 'Properties, Modalities, and God', *Philosophical Review*, 93 (1984) pp. 35–56.
41. Fischer, 'Freedom and Foreknowledge', p. 76.
42. Ibid., pp. 76–7.
43. Richard Swinburne, *The Coherence of Theism* (Oxford: Oxford University Press, 1977) p. 170.

4 The Nature of God's Knowledge

1. Augustine, *De Trinitate*, XV, 13.
2. Thomas Aquinas, *Summa Theologia*, Ia, 14, 8.

3. Charles Adams and Paul Tannery (eds) *Oeuvres de Descartes*, 12 volumes (Paris: Leopold Cerg, 1897–1910) vol. I, p. 147.
4. That a view of this sort might be possible is defended in Thomas V. Morris's recent piece, 'Necessary Beings', *Mind*, 94 (1985) pp. 263–72.
5. I intend the notion of bringing about to be understood so that there are no causally sufficient conditions for an action in question when a person can be properly said to have brought about something.
6 An excellent discussion of Molina's views can be found in Robert Adams, 'Middle Knowledge and the Problem of Evil', *American Philosophical Quarterly*, 14 (1977) pp. 109–17.
7. Ibid.
8. David Lewis, 'Causation', in Sosa (ed.) *Causation and Conditionals* (Oxford: Oxford University Press, 1975). Lewis's views on the role that miracles play in evaluating which worlds are closest to the actual one are developed further in 'Counterfactual Dependence and Time's Arrow', *Nous*, 13 (1979) pp. 455–76. For further discussion of the issues surrounding Lewis's appeal to miracles, cf. Jonathan Bennett, 'Counterfactuals and Temporal Direction', *Philosophical Review*, 93 (1984) pp. 57–91.
9. Marshall Swain, *Reasons and Knowledge* (Ithaca: Cornell University Press) pp. 58–65.
10. Cf. Adams's account of Suarez's position in 'Middle Knowledge'.
11. Adams, p. 110. I have altered his numbering of propositions in this passage and in the others which I shall quote to accord with mine.
12. Ibid.
13.· Ibid.
14. Ibid., p. 111.
15. Ibid.
16. Adams gives the following locations for counter-examples to the law of CEM: Lewis, *Counterfactuals*, pp. 79f., and John Pollock, 'Four Kinds of Conditionals', *American Philosophical Quarterly*, 12 (1975) p. 53.
17. Adams, p. 111.
18. Adams, p. 110.
19. Note that the 'because' in these explanations is not causal.
20. Anthony Kenny, *The God of the Philosophers* (Oxford: Oxford University Press, 1979).
21. Ibid., pp. 68–71.
22. Adams, pp. 113–14.
23. Ibid., p. 114.
24. Ibid.

5 Omniscience, Omnipresence, Immutability and Timelessness

1. Norman Kretzmann, 'Omniscience and Immutability', *Journal of Philosophy*, 63 (1966) pp. 409–21.
2. Cf. Arthur Prior, 'The Formalities of Omniscience', *Philosophy* 37 (1962); Nicholas Woltersdorff, 'God Everlasting', pp. 77–98 in *Contem-*

porary Philosophy of Religion, edited by Steven Cahn and David Shatz (New York: Oxford University Press,1982).

3. Prior, 'The Formalities of Omniscience'.

4. Wolterstorff, 'God Everlasting'.

5. Anthony Kenny, 'Divine Foreknowledge and Human Freedom', in Kenny (ed.) *Aquinas, A Collection of Critical Essays* (Notre Dame: University of Notre Dame Press, 1976) p. 264.

6. For a recent investigation and defence of this response to the simultaneity objection to the coherence of the timelessness doctrine, see Eleonore Stump and Norman Kretzmann, 'Eternity', *The Journal of Philosophy* 78 (1981) pp. 429–58.

7   William P. Alston, 'Divine–Human Dialogue and the Nature of God', *Faith and Philosophy*, 2 (1985) p. 13. The view that Alston explicates is Aquinas's view in, e.g., *Summa Contra Gentiles*, II, 35–6. This view is carefully explained as well in Stump and Kretzmann, 'Eternity', pp. 447–50.

Index